"This is the perfect book to give someone
who is embarking on the adventure of therapy.
It is also models to the rest of us—
both professional and nonprofessional—
how therapy should be!
A public dialogue that will help many."

PATRICK J. CARNES, PH.D., CAS

HEALING CONVERSATIONS

THERAPY & SPIRITUAL GROWTH

Dorothy Barnes & Ralph Earle

InterVarsity Press
Downers Grove, Illinois

InterVarsity Press
P.O. Box 1400, Downers Grove, IL 60515
World Wide Web: www.ivpress.com
E-mail: mail@ivpress.com

InterVarsity Press® *is the book-publishing division of InterVarsity Christian Fellowship/USA*®, *a
student movement active on campus at hundreds of universities, colleges and schools of nursing in the
United States of America, and a member movement of the International Fellowship of Evangelical
Students. For information about local and regional activities, write Public Relations Dept.,
InterVarsity Christian Fellowship/USA, 6400 Schroeder Rd., P.O. Box 7895, Madison, WI 53707-7895.*

All Scripture quotations, unless otherwise indicated, are taken from the Holy Bible, New International
Version®. NIV®. *Copyright ©1973, 1978, 1984 by International Bible Society. Used by permission of
Zondervan Publishing House. All rights reserved.*

Cover photograph: Michael Goss

ISBN 0-8308-1948-7

Printed in the United States of America ♾

Library of Congress Cataloging-in-Publication Data

Barnes, Dorothy (Dorothy J.)
    Healing conversations : therapy and spiritual growth / Dorothy
Barnes and Ralph Earle.
        p.   cm.
    Includes bibliographical references.
    ISBN 0-8308-1948-7 (pbk. : alk. paper)
    1. Psychotherapy—Popular works.   2. Psychotherapy—Case studies
3. Psychotherapy—Religious aspects—Christianity.   I. Earle, Ralph
(Ralph H.)   II. Title.
RC480.515.B37   1998
616.89'14—dc21   *98-13663*
                                                                        CIP

19	18	17	16	15	14	13	12	11	10	9	8	7	6	5	4	3	2	1
14	13	12	11	10	09	08	07	06	05	04	03	02	01	00	99	98		

96596

My affection, respect and gratitude are given
to the many people involved in supporting this book
and me, including my friends,
writers' group and the staff at InterVarsity Press.
I dedicate this book to my husband, John,
and our three fabulous children,
Celeste, Dan and Julie.

DOROTHY

Warm thanks to my wife, Glenda, our children
and grandchildren, and to our colleagues,
both clergy and therapists, who join us in the integration
of spirituality and therapy.

RALPH

Introduction
—Dorothy—

This book invites you to look at the process of recovery through the eyes of a patient (Dorothy) and her therapist (Ralph). It describes the therapy experience I had with psychologist Ralph Earle. All of the facts and events described in these pages are real.

The roof of our house had been leaking for over a year. We live in a desert area where it's easy to ignore this problem because it rains so seldom. When the rains came, we positioned buckets under the drips.

Our attempts to patch the roof only resulted in new leaks. We were frustrated because we couldn't locate the source of the leaks. After one heavy rainfall, a large bubble began to form in our son's bedroom ceiling. With each rainfall it grew larger.

Eventually we had to dry out parts of the ceiling and replace wet insulation—major repairs. Since we were unable to pinpoint the leak, we covered over every imaginable place where leakage could occur. Then we waited.

When rain fell again, the roof seemed to hold and we began to relax. Then a heavy winter storm resulted in a new crack in our bedroom ceiling. We stared in disbelief. Where was the water coming from?

Finally we called a roofing specialist, who told us exactly what we didn't want to hear: we needed a new roof. Expensive news. The damaged roof was crying out to us, "Pay attention to me! Quit trying to ignore my dysfunction! I need help!"

The roofers finally found the original leak under the air conditioner. The rotten boards and support structures had nearly collapsed under the heavy cooling unit. Eventually the supports would have given way, allowing the air conditioner to fall into the house.

As the story of the leaky roof probably demonstrates, I am reluctant to ask for help when I need it, especially when I can't identify the specific problem or when I think I should have the answer. Perhaps you have a difficult time too. When you are in a strange city, do you refuse to ask for directions until you are hopelessly lost? When you are sad or angry, do you wear a smile and tell the world you're fine? Are you lonely and distrustful—surrounded by many and known by few?

Our spiritual and emotional health tends to be wrapped in an aura of mystery. When we experience problems in these areas, we may try to fix them ourselves. But our attempts often leave us frustrated and defeated, as my husband and I were when we tried to fix our roof. Sometimes we wait too long to get help, and our world does indeed come crashing in around us. Or maybe we deny our problems. Denial and other defense mechanisms such as repression, perfectionism, addiction and avoidance allow us to hide from our own dysfunction.

One help that is available is therapy. Unfortunately, many people see therapy as an option for others but not for themselves. They watch people go through therapy without changes in anything other than their wallets. Other people see therapy as a crutch, not a solution. Some view it as an admission of weakness. I initially recoiled at the thought of seeking therapy. I thought it was for people who couldn't work out their own problems.

I have always been an easy person for others to confide in. But the reason I developed good listening skills was to avoid revealing anything of myself to others. I became highly skilled at concealing my self. But these "personal relationships" were draining me. I felt exhausted.

Did I go into therapy to work through those relationship problems? No. I went for many different reasons. I wanted to deepen my relationship with God, look at my fears, explore my past to see how it was affecting my present and learn to help family members deal with some of their problems.

The pages in this book describe my therapy sessions and the work that therapy required. The word *work* is key. If you go into therapy thinking that someone will wave a magic wand and you will be fixed (or others will be fixed), you are in for shock and disappointment. If you really want therapy to succeed, you will work hard during therapy sessions and do your homework between sessions.

The most important member of my therapy team was God. Each person's experience of knowing God is personal and intimate, and I am not trying to prescribe a formula that works for everyone. But you don't have to share my beliefs to witness the power of God in my therapy.

There were times when I laughed in therapy and times when I cried. There were times when I left my therapist in anger, vowing never to return to him. And there were times when life never seemed better. Ultimately my journey led me to a better place. Join me!

—Ralph's Notes—

What do you think and feel as you approach a roller coaster at an amusement park? Excitement laced with apprehension? Putting your trust in those who operate the ride can be scary. Anticipating the scary plunges and hairy twists may produce anxiety. You may or may not breathe a sigh of relief as the ride comes to an end.

In many ways therapy is like that roller coaster. Excitement and apprehension are normal emotions for new clients approaching their first counseling session. (The terms *client* and *patient* are used interchangeably throughout the book to reflect the terminology used by different therapists.) They may have many questions about the therapy and the therapist. It's important for patients to find a therapist they can trust to guide them through the ups and downs inherent in the process of learning who they are.

Therapy mimics life and can be difficult at times. Therapy gives patients an opportunity to experience the roller coaster of life in a different way. They can try out new behaviors without being rejected or abandoned. Therapy is a safe place to explore beliefs and feelings. This book describes the roller-coaster ride of therapy as it evolved for one patient, Dorothy, and for me as her therapist.

Who Is Ralph?

I am in the business of helping people more fully experience their life journey through the process of therapy. I bring my training as a psychologist and ordained minister as well as my own experience to the process. Knowing something about me will, I hope, help you understand how I approach the therapy process.

My story begins in Boston, where I was born on April 2, 1937. I was the only child of two ordained Nazarene ministers. I lived most of my childhood in Kansas City, Missouri. My Christian religion formed the backdrop for everything as I was growing up. There were both advantages and drawbacks in that.

The advantages included a large, loving support system that began with my parents and involved others in my church and extended family. My parents and I traveled a great deal because of their speaking engagements. By the time I was fourteen, we had visited every state. I enjoy traveling to this day.

My father and mother imparted to me a taste for academic pursuits. I enjoyed my college and university experiences, which included Pasadena College (now Point Loma Nazarene University), Edinburgh University in Scotland (New College), Nazarene Theological Seminary, Harvard Divinity School and the School of Theology, Claremont. I still enjoy learning as well as teaching and writing.

My religious background was highly structured and very controlled. We had daily family devotions in which we prayed for, in my opinion, half of the Nazarene missionaries in the world. My parents encouraged me to study the Bible. I memorized Scripture verses primarily for the cash reward my parents gave me. Many of those verses remain in my mind to this day, and I often retrieve them when I need to.

The drawbacks were the restrictions and rules that our particular Christian movement enforced. I wasn't allowed to dance, play cards, join high-school fraternities or go to movies. Once I went to a movie with a friend instead of going to a Boy Scout event. The movie was *Sorry, Wrong Number.* The title led us to believe that God was speaking directly through our choice of movies. I never saw another movie until I graduated from college.

My parents loved me very much. Our family members hugged each other a lot, particularly my mom. At times my mom's hugging felt like smothering because she hugged so much. My dad was more aloof.

I met Glenda, my wife, in Prescott, Arizona. We were married on June 6, 1958. Our two children, Marcus and Michelle, were born in 1961 and 1963 respectively. I have been involved in three types of therapy as a patient. I have had individual therapy, Glenda and I have done couples therapy, and I have participated with the four of us in family therapy.

In the course of my life I have been a parish minister, an author and a family psychologist. As I progressed through my theological journey, I chose a counseling ministry as opposed to a pulpit ministry. It has always been important for me, as a therapist, to help people integrate their spiritual side with the other areas of their life.

I have addressed the spiritual side of people's lives more often as a therapist than I ever did as a minister. For nearly thirty years I have helped patients deal with the spiritual side of their lives without being hampered by the restrictions sometimes associated with working within a particular denomination. My patients are freed up to do their own journeys in the way that is most therapeutically sound for them.

Over the years I have written several books. I have addressed numerous gatherings as a guest speaker, and I have appeared on many television and radio programs. But the experience I enjoy most is the time I spend with patients, working with them to promote growth and healing in their lives.

When I am not working, I love spending time with my five grandchildren: Brianna, Andrew, Sarah, Chase and Cade. They have dubbed me "Cuckoo." I always laugh when they come into the building and shout at the top of their lungs, "Where's Cuckoo?" Then when I come out of my office, they shout, "There's Cuckoo!" Patients look up and smile their approval of the moniker.

Why This Book?

I believe in reading books as part of the therapy process. Some of the important work of therapy is completed outside of the session. Reading books can be a vital link between sessions for client and therapist. It's common for me to recommend books to people to help move the therapy process forward. Many self-help books are available for additional education and support during therapy.

This book provides both therapists and patients the opportunity to look inside the process. For therapists, it's a resource to reflect on what's similar and what's dissimilar in their own practice—a book in which they can identify and reflect on the things that worked and the things that didn't. It's not very often that therapists have an opportunity to sit down and review the whole process of therapy. Some reflection takes place at the end of each patient's therapy, but it's usually to assess how the patient is doing, not to review the sessions.

For the patients or potential patients who are looking at the process of therapy, this book provides a view of Dorothy's sessions that is intended to demystify the process. New patients are often confused or frightened because they don't understand what is going to happen. They don't know what to expect or what questions to ask.

As a therapist, I do the best I can in each moment and try to be clear about that as I counsel patients. "Ralph's Notes" describe my perceptions, feelings and decisions as Dorothy's therapist. They reflect my therapy choices and decisions as they related to Dorothy. This book is a unique opportunity for me to share, in retrospect, my own thoughts and feelings about being in the role of therapist.

Therapy and Spirituality
In this book Dorothy utilizes prayer as a safe and comfortable way to communicate with herself and God. During the toughest times in therapy, writing prayers often kept Dorothy in the process when she wanted to quit or run away. Through prayer Dorothy opened up more deeply to herself. I believe prayer helped make therapy safe for her. I do not routinely have people use Bible reading or prayer in every counseling session. Some counselors do. When prayers can function as an open door to the soul, they enhance the therapeutic process.

Written prayer became Dorothy's form of journaling. It was introspective and very real. Prayer is an important part of my own life, so it served as a link between us.

Some therapists, unfortunately, are closed to patients' spirituality. In the past if a patient shared a prayer with a therapist, the response might have been "It's irrelevant," or "Would you please use other language to describe what you are talking about?" Most therapists were not open to spiritual exploration in the process of counseling.

In recent years the therapeutic profession has become more open toward spirituality. Some professionals are willing to embrace spiritual questions and beliefs as part of the integration of a person. There's an openness to explore and actively pursue a patient's faith and how that faith is being used in the present. It is critically important that a person's spirituality start where the person is. The therapist always affirms the patients' right to do what is most helpful for them.

It's equally unfortunate when patients' spirituality closes them to the therapy process. Sadly, some religious people believe that therapy is inappropriate for spiritual reasons. They refuse to find in it a solution for the problem of emotional pain. Their message is that digging deeper and praying harder will drive away anxiety and pain. Professional guidance is considered unnecessary.

I hope this book will encourage people to seek help. As a professional therapist, I hope that more therapists will deal with spirituality issues. Dorothy and I look forward to sharing our journey with you. I believe that every therapy process gives birth to a story. At the very least, a new chapter is written in the lives of the participants.

1

First Encounters
—*Dorothy*—

W *hat should I wear? What if I can't go through with it? Should I tell him everything he wants to know? What if someone recognizes me?* My mind raced. Fears washed over me like waves battering the shore. I had two hours to make up my mind. Only two hours? Could I do this? Should I? What would happen to me?

This had to be kept secret. Anyone who saw me with him might jump to the wrong conclusions. If only he had a secret entrance for persons who wanted, who needed, to remain anonymous. Why isn't there a guidebook that explains all of this?

The dilemma I faced at that moment was choosing an outfit to wear. Emily Post never discussed what to wear for this type of meeting. Meeting? Would it actually be a "meeting"? Or was I about to enter a torture chamber?

What was I expected to wear to this meeting? Black suit and white silk blouse? Too conservative: "She's rigid." Since Christmas was approaching, how about a green sweater and black slacks? No, I was in Arizona. I might be too warm in a sweater. I might perspire and he might think I was anxious. My goal was to sell him on the idea that I was perfectly normal—no quirks, no deviant personality problems, no hysteria, no depression, no addictions. I was simply experiencing some anxiety and some fears that I had never felt before and I wanted to be free of. I estimated it would take three sessions—maximum—to accomplish my goal.

My white suit with a red blouse? Gold cross pendant, wedding ring, tennis bracelet and earrings to complete the image. Professional but fun. It is much easier to dress when you aren't trying to use your clothes to make a personality statement.

By the time I was ready to go, some of my confidence had returned. I was good at shaping my appearance to present a confident exterior. If only I could control what was going on inside me—nagging fears, sleeplessness, strange feelings, *no feelings.*

What about *him?* Was he a person of integrity? How would I inquire about confidentiality issues without appearing paranoid? Was he trustworthy? Most people weren't. I'd be able to tell. But what if he was an exception?

Or what if he decided not to work with me? What if *I* didn't measure up to *his* criteria? I had checked his credentials and had spoken with people who knew him. But I never thought he might decide against seeing me. New fears joined old ones. Stuff them deep inside with all the rest. What else was there to do?

It was unlike me to fear something new. I liked adventure and the excitement of challenging situations. But I was beset by a vague sense that something was wrong in my life. When I slowed down enough to think about it, I detected a feeling of uneasiness that sometimes grew into a sense of urgency and wouldn't go away.

A thirty-minute drive to Scottsdale brought me to Psychological Counseling Services (PCS) for my appointment. I was early. As I sat in my car, I gazed at the clinic and willed myself to go in. The single-story building housed only the counseling center. A casual onlooker would know that anyone going in there was seeing a therapist.

Gathering my courage, I got out of my car and walked to the entrance. Two massive wooden doors were the last barrier to my going inside. As I opened them, I noticed a large Christmas wreath on one of the waiting room walls. There were bright, shiny ornaments on it, and there was a beautiful gold ribbon woven through it. Seeing this decoration comforted me.

In the waiting room several people sat in silence. When I looked around, several eyes met mine and then glanced away. Good! They didn't want to be noticed any more than I did. I walked to the front counter to sign in, or whatever it is you do at your first visit to a psychologist. "Hello, my name is Dorothy Barnes, and I'm here to see Dr. Earle."

"Which Dr. Earle?" came the reply from the person guarding the office area.

"Dr. Ralph Earle," I answered. I had forgotten that his son worked in the same office. I hoped for an end to the questioning. I wanted to get the paperwork filled out so that I could sit down.

"Please complete these forms and bring them back when you are finished." She handed them to me and returned to work.

I sat in a bluish-gray chair facing the lovely wreath. Identical straight-backed chairs lined three walls. I had a view of the hallway that I assumed led to the doctors' offices. The room was very quiet except for the occasional ringing of the phone.

The forms I was given to fill out included the usual questions about insurance coverage and personal information. There was also a statement of confidentiality. Filling in the blanks was easy, and I didn't have to describe symptoms or give reasons for being there. As I wrote, I wondered about the people sitting silently around me. Some read magazines, others stared into space, and a few chatted together quietly.

I turned in the completed paperwork and waited for further instructions. Nothing. The person behind the desk thanked me and returned to work. The best thing to do when you don't know what to do is to copy what everyone else is doing. So I sat and surveyed the room. Even when I am frightened, I like to explore and discover. So I put fears on hold and looked around, carefully avoiding any eye contact.

A coffee table held stacks of popular magazines. Pamphlets and brochures offered information about therapy groups and workshops. Next to the front doors hung a picture composed of red, black and white squares filled with objects and phrases. It reminded me of something you might see in a museum. Two framed prints from the Art Institute of Chicago were centered on adjacent walls, and a painting of the American West decorated a far wall at the end of a hallway.

The room was too quiet. It needed some classical music. In ten minutes my appointment would begin. The phone rang. Appointments were made and canceled, and still the patients waited. Then, as if on cue, there was movement—doors opened, voices chattered. People came walking down the hallway toward the waiting room. Some of them left the building, and others stopped at the front desk. Still others went into the office area to retrieve messages and grab files.

The doctors were not dressed in white coats. They said goodbye to their patients and then slipped into a side door. Apparently every session ended at the same time. I looked for Dr. Earle, thinking that I could recognize him from having attended a lecture of his. The waiting room was now empty except for me.

"Dorothy, Ralph Earle; nice to meet you." He seemed to have entered the room from nowhere. He shook my hand and invited me to follow him to his office. I liked our initial contact, and I was provisionally pleased with my decision to see him.

Ralph Earle was tall and energetic. He moved rapidly and smiled when he talked. I had expected him to be dressed in a suit, but he was wearing a sweater and dress slacks. He was easy to be with, although I still feared the process. We passed a water cooler with a plant on it and turned left at the cowboy picture.

"Please, have a seat wherever you like." Suddenly I was facing a predicament—what seat should I choose? I thought he might be watching me. Perhaps my choice would reflect on me in some way. His office was large and contained two swivel chairs, a couch, a desk chair and his chair, which was different from the other chairs and was facing them. It was a large, cushioned rattan chair that was out of sync with the room decor. His interior decorator must have been overruled on the chair.

I decided against the couch. It was too far away, and it had a certain stereotypical stigma attached to it. The desk chair was located away from the grouping and was out of the question. Either swivel chair would do. I took the one closest to the door. Just in case! He closed the door as I was seated, and then he sat in his rattan chair.

The quiet reasserted itself as Dr. Earle read through my file. Then he looked up at me and smiled. "Dorothy, tell me why you're here and how I can help you." Great smile—safe smile. I didn't know the answer to either question but decided I'd better say something—anything.

"For the past year I've been afraid of some things I haven't been afraid of before." He was writing. What did I say? What did he write? I felt vulnerable about my life being captured in handwritten notes.

"Go on." He put his pen down.

I continued, "I have three children, and I fear for the youngest, who is eight. I am afraid to let her play at the park or leave her when I travel. I'd also like to improve some relationships in my extended family and deepen my relationship with God."

"Tell me about your relationship with God," he encouraged.

"My relationship with God is the most important one I have. What I don't have is a 'feeling' of love toward God. I do love God intentionally, but I don't feel it. Many people talk about their passion for God and their feelings toward God. I don't have that but I want it. I've prayed, read books, watched others, and I just don't have the feelings." Ralph leaned forward and listened intently to what I said. Having someone listen to me felt strange. I usually did all of the listening. I'm very good at listening.

"Tell me more about how you pray."

Here was an area I was passionate about. "I write my prayers," I answered.

"How often?" he asked.

"Every day."

I was glad to talk about my relationship with God. It was important for me to have a therapist who was open to the spiritual side of who I am. I didn't need a therapist who believed exactly what I believed, but I did need one who was open to my understanding. Ralph Earle is an ordained minister as well as a therapist, so I had expectations about his being open to spiritual issues. But I didn't want a therapist who would dictate theology to me. I watched carefully to see if he would do that. So far he hadn't.

"Would you please bring me a week's worth of your written prayers the next time you come in?" he requested.

So I was coming back, and I had homework to do. That meant that I had passed the "test" and he would continue to see me. He had passed the test with me too. I liked Ralph. He was very kind and direct.

We covered a lot of ground during that initial session, including my goals for being in therapy. I had approached therapy in a state of confusion. As I verbalized my needs with Ralph, I was able to clarify them in my own mind. Articulating what troubled me helped me sort through the uneasiness I felt. It helped to give words to the unsettled feelings I had lived with.

My goals for therapy included looking at my past, dealing with my fears, working on current relationships and enjoying an intimate relationship with God. How and when that work would take place was unclear to me, but I had decided that the time I spent in therapy was my gift to me. I was determined to focus on myself in a concentrated and purposeful way. I wanted to experience a safe place to be truthful about who I was and what I wanted to become.

Truthfulness was a promise that I made to myself before I chose therapy. I made a decision to be as open as possible. Somehow I knew transparency was crucial to my ability to grow. I considered myself a truthful and honest person, but I knew how to be silent and how to avoid areas that frightened me or seemed best forgotten. Inwardly I made a vow to answer anything I was asked and to explore any area that came up.

"Dorothy, please tell me some things you like about yourself," Ralph continued.

"I think I am smart, funny and creative. I play the piano and I'm a good mother and wife." I hadn't expected that question, but it was fun—light. I didn't find it difficult to come up with likable things about myself. I thought everyone had good qualities. I was a positive person most of the time, although I had high standards, especially for myself.

"I think you're a fun person too." Ralph was generous with expressions of kindness and encouragement. It wasn't long before I became engrossed in our conversation and forgot my fear of the process. "Dorothy, I see that you were referred by your pastor. I would like to write to him to let him know we met. When a pastor or another therapist refers someone to me, I usually send that person a follow-up letter. Is that all right with you?" He waited for my reply.

Fear swept over me. I felt uncomfortable letting anyone know me on a deeply personal level. My friends and acquaintances often confided in me, but I controlled what I shared about myself. I had not told anyone that I was seeking therapy except for my pastor, my husband John, and my friend Connie. I hadn't even told my children. I didn't mind my pastor's knowing, but did he have to know in writing? This letter would go through many hands before it reached him, and many people would have access to it.

As I debated the issue with myself, Ralph jumped up and walked to his desk. He returned to where I sat with a form for me to sign that gave him permission to write to my pastor. I took the form and read it over carefully. I never sign anything without examining every word, especially if it puts me at risk for something—in this case, exposure. That has been a source of endless annoyance for salespeople. The form Ralph gave me to sign was short and specific. Finally I decided to trust his judgment and signed the form, even though something inside of me screamed, *Don't sign! It's not safe.*

"Dorothy, what people do you trust?" My struggle over the permission slip must have triggered his question.

I had to think a moment before I answered. "I trust my husband John, my pastor, my father-in-law and my friend Connie." My response required deliberation and thought. I wondered if my list was longer or shorter than other people's.

"You mentioned a concern about your anger. Times when you thought you overreacted to a situation. Tell me about a time when you had that kind of anger."

"When I was in college, I received a full scholarship to a master's degree program, along with fellowship monies that allowed me to attend school without the extra burden of working. I was a single parent at that time, and the coursework was demanding. One day a professor I liked and trusted accused me of leaving a coffee cup in the clinic area. She said it was unprofessional and unlike me." I hesitated.

"Go on, please."

"Well, I hadn't left a coffee cup anywhere. I didn't even drink coffee. Even though I knew this was a minor incident, I reacted with hurricane force. After a few days of being angry I quit the program. I think I used the coffee incident as an escape from the stress of attending school." I felt stupid relaying this past incident.

"So you shot yourself in the foot because of your anger," he replied.

"Yes, that's exactly what I did."

Ralph went on to question me about the other areas of my life that I had mentioned to him. We discussed my extended family and my take on those relationships. We talked about my immediate family situation. With every statistic or fact, he gently pushed for more information. Facts were not enough. He wanted the feelings associated with the relationship. I was most comfortable furnishing statistical information about my family and friends. I wasn't uncomfortable about my feelings toward them, but I had difficulty verbalizing them. I felt disconnected, unable to identify with what he asked of me.

"Our time is almost up for today. Is there anything else you'd like to tell me, or are there any questions you'd like to ask?" Ralph closed my file and moved forward in his seat, as if ready to stand up. I hadn't noticed him looking at his watch or glancing at the clock sitting on an end table. I didn't have any further questions. My mind was too full of the newness of this experience to handle any more input.

"I'd like for you to have the next several sessions with other doctors here in the building. We do that for two reasons. First, it gives you a chance to experience different therapists to see which one you want to end up working with. Second, it allows you to complete several therapy processes with the specialist in that area. You will be completing a genogram, which is similar to a family history, and a trauma egg drawing that depicts traumatic events in your life and the feelings associated with them. I will see you after that." Ralph stood as he outlined my treatment plan.

Other therapists! I didn't want to see other therapists! It never once entered my mind that I would have to talk to a team of people. This was definitely not OK with me. "Why can't you do what they do?"

"I can, but they are particularly skilled in those areas. The thought of talking to someone else makes you anxious, doesn't it?"

"Yes," I replied softly. As Ralph described the therapists and the procedures in greater detail, I became more comfortable with the idea.

"I've enjoyed getting to know you today. You have a lot of courage, and I look forward to our working together if I make sense for you as a therapist." The expression on my face must have suggested that I questioned his sincerity. "I mean that," he said. We left the office, and he walked with me to the invisible spot in the hallway where patient and doctor separate. He went into the office space, and I went to the desk to pay for my session. The changing-of-the-guard dance was reenacted, and I was part of it.

—*Ralph's Notes*—

Looking back, I find it interesting that Dorothy spent so much time deciding what to wear. As a therapist, I think about what I'm going to wear, especially when I have a speaking date. A guidebook would be of use to Dorothy. One of the things I enjoy about having a practice in Scottsdale is the flexibility in dressing, which means I don't always wear a shirt and tie.

I've had male patients who came in wearing a shirt and tie when I was wearing a sport shirt. At the next appointment they wore a sport shirt, and I was wearing a shirt and tie. They have expressed confusion regarding this area, and sometimes they have apologized for wearing the "wrong" clothes. But there is no dress code. A patient who has a challenge in the area of sexual addiction may dress inappropriately. We then discuss that as a therapeutic issue in session. But otherwise choice of clothing is strictly a nonissue.

Dorothy's experience of racing thoughts leads me to the realization that patients think about many things before their sessions. New patients may indeed feel considerable anxiety as they contemplate beginning therapy. I need to remain aware of that as I see new patients. Such anxiety has even led some patients to cancel their appointments.

Length of Therapy

Dorothy mentioned her intention to sell me on the idea that she was "normal." I hear that frequently from patients. Many patients try to sell me on either of two extremes: that they are "perfectly normal" or "perfectly abnormal."

Dorothy's intention to accomplish her goals in three sessions is challenging. I used to pride myself on the brief therapy that I did—eight to twelve sessions. That has radically changed due to the long-term nature of addictions and challenging family-of-origin issues. Some patients simply need more help than can be provided in a brief therapy model.

Brief therapy is sometimes useful in addressing sexual issues such as premature ejaculation and in improving communication in marriage. It can also be useful with behavior modification, since insight is not as necessary, for example, helping a person identify an anger cycle. My goal is to keep therapy as brief as possible in the patient's best interest. Brevity, besides being the soul of wit, is a current trend in therapy due to requirements made by managed care and insurance companies.

Confidentiality and Trust

Dorothy is a very private person and was concerned about confidentiality and trust. I had the impression, very early on, that she was going to test me to see whether or not it made sense to open up to me. We were not going to get anywhere if I couldn't prove to her that I could be trusted. I like that. Candor is an honest kind of approach, whereas somebody who is very smooth and talkative may seem open without actually being open.

Dorothy made it clear, even during her first session, that she would not open up until she trusted me. A lot of our process, in the beginning, revolved around her deciding whether or not to share her innermost thoughts with me. It takes tremendous trust for a patient to reveal her or his self to me or to any therapist, for that matter.

Sharing the Process

In the beginning Dorothy expressed most of her feelings in the prayers she wrote. After a month or two of sessions I made a comment that Dorothy's prayers were good enough to be published. Dorothy took my suggestion to heart because she cares deeply about her faith. Then she decided to include a description of her therapy process as well. Dorothy proposed writing this book as a joint venture after her therapy terminated. The project turned into a yearlong exploration of issues involving ethics and confidentiality.

I gave thought to Dorothy's proposal, discussed it with the staff here at PCS and consulted people outside of our group practice. We decided that I should wait one year after Dorothy's therapy ended before participating in any way on the book project. The decision to wait a year was made after therapy had actually been terminated. Dorothy researched possible risks involved in our working on a joint venture. Therapists are bound by ethical codes and laws designed to protect their patients. I have described our decision-making process in some detail because of those confidentiality and patient-doctor issues.

Presenting Problem

In our first session Dorothy mentioned a vague sense of something being wrong in her life. Many of my patients make initial statements about not knowing why they are seeking therapy. I think it was very natural for Dorothy to feel some dread because she feared the whole process.

My goal as a therapist was to help Dorothy identify goals for her therapy, to help her decide whether or not it made sense to continue.

In some cases I've helped patients come to the realization that therapy probably didn't make sense at that time.

The Waiting Room

It's interesting that Dorothy noticed the large Christmas wreath in our waiting room. The ambiance of the setting, "the presentation," is part of doing therapy. The goal is to make the setting peaceful and comfortable. We want our setting to encourage opening up.

Dorothy mentioned that several people in the waiting room looked at her and then glanced away. Her assumption that they did not want her to notice them any more than she wanted them to notice her may or may not be accurate. It's my belief that having other people around helps with desensitization, whereas secrecy promotes fear.

Vanessa, the receptionist at our front desk, is very important to the therapy process. She is friendly and caring and is a tremendous resource to someone who is hurting. Patients refer to her as their friend. We at Psychological Counseling Services are blessed to have someone who establishes rapport quickly with patients.

Forms to Be Filled Out

As Dorothy waited for her session to begin, she was asked to fill out some forms. The treatment agreement helped Dorothy understand the rules, the regulations and the therapeutic contract. It includes statements regarding confidentiality, hours and availability, fees and payment. Patients are asked to sign the form confirming that they have reviewed the information and agree to the terms of the treatment procedures. I want patients to ask me about anything they don't understand.

The new patient information form compiles demographic information about the patient. It's a single-page data form. There are no diagnostic questions on either form. Diagnostic questions are not addressed until the patient is in session with the therapist.

Rapport

Dorothy and I succeeded in establishing rapport during the first appointment. I always go out to meet my patients, and I went out front to meet Dorothy. I do that for every appointment. I introduced myself, and we went back to my office. I was curious about Dorothy, as I am with all new patients. I wondered why she was here and how I could help.

First Session

The first session actually began in the waiting room, as our initial contact occurred before we entered my office. Dorothy's interest in the process, as well as her anxiety, were apparent even as she waited to meet me. I didn't ask Dorothy why she had come to me until we were in my office. I never ask patients how they're doing, even though that is a typical greeting. When a patient asks how I'm doing, I don't ask back. The patient might be horrified to think that we were going to start discussing his or her problem publicly.

Usually my information about a new patient is limited. In Dorothy's case, I assumed she was a female patient because of her name. I noticed that she was well dressed when I first saw her. As we began to talk in my office, she showed herself to be articulate, intelligent and anxious.

Dorothy's anxiety extended to choosing a chair to sit in. I do not care where anyone sits. I'm in the office eight to nine hours at a time, so I like to sit in a variety of chairs. Patients sometimes ask if their choice is somehow making a statement about themselves. I do notice where clients sit, but I don't attach any meaning to it without checking that out with them.

Telling Her Story

When Dorothy came to my office, I knew nothing about her story. Thus the first question I asked was "Why are you here?" Patients often respond with "I expected you to ask a question like that." Some patients answer, "I don't know why I'm here." Then I respond with "I have no idea why you're here either, so we're starting off at the same level: neither one of us knows why you're here. I think it's your turn to talk now because I'm a therapist, not a psychic." Usually this provokes a laugh, and we start talking to see what comes up.

With Dorothy I looked for two types of information. First, I'm listening for her story, and second, I'm making a decision about my being the right person to help her with her problem. The content of her story may suggest that someone else could be more helpful to her. In that case I would suggest a referral to another therapist.

As I listened to Dorothy's story, I wanted her to know I understood as much as I could about her reasons for seeking therapy. I gave her feedback to confirm that I had heard her correctly. When she got most of her presenting problem (reason for coming to therapy) out, we talked about how I thought we could help her.

Goals
One of the reasons I decided to take Dorothy on as a patient was her goal of deepening her relationship with God. All of our therapists here at PCS recognize the importance of addressing the spiritual lives of our patients. I have no interest in promoting any particular theological framework.

Dorothy said she didn't have any "feelings" toward God. For me, prayer is about feelings and relationships. I wanted to know what prayer meant for her. Her remark about writing her prayers every day caught my attention. In a later session, when I first read one of her prayers, it was clear to me her prayers were very much a feeling exercise.

When I came to know Dorothy better, I understood that Dorothy's God was one who loved her and was loved by her.

Praying to God meant talking to God about what was going on in her life. The more prayers she wrote, the better she expressed her range of feelings in therapy.

It appeared, even in the first session, that her relationship with God was her safest relationship. As her therapist, I appreciated that later she allowed me to get to know her through sharing her prayers. Since she was such a private person, her prayers were what provided a window into her soul. Although she had stated that having an intimate relationship with God was one of her goals, my hunch was that she already had a deeply intimate relationship with God. The goal was to help her recognize the existence of that intimacy and understand that she could also establish healthy intimacy with safe people, including her husband, John.

Dorothy's candor expresses itself well in her unusual dialogue with God. Dorothy tapped into the resource of written prayer very powerfully as a way of doing therapy.

Being Transparent

I did not know at the time that Dorothy had made a decision during our first session to be transparent in therapy. That's an essential part of doing therapy. One of my responsibilities as a therapist with Dorothy was to encourage her to let me know what was going on in her mind. In later sessions when she was stuck or afraid, I would say something like "Dorothy, you can say anything to me that you would say to yourself." That is not the way most of us have been programmed.

I realized almost immediately Dorothy could talk about her thoughts more easily than her feelings. In the beginning the therapy process was focused on her thoughts. The goal, as soon as possible, was for me to be a person who made sense for Dorothy to open up to and share as much as she knew about herself.

When I asked Dorothy to identify some things she liked about herself, she could do that. I always ask patients to name positive things about themselves in a first session. Some patients answer, "Hey, that's why I'm here. I don't like anything about myself." Then I ask them to tell me something other people like about them. I want all patients to get in touch with something redemptive about themselves.

Trust

Every time I asked Dorothy to sign a form, she scrutinized and sometimes revised the wording, which was great. She signed revised forms that we were both comfortable with. In the first session I asked her to sign a form that allowed me to include her pastor in the process. My request provided us with an opportunity to look at her fears. If we found that a release of information form was not in her best interest, she and I would both vote against it.

Her pastor was already on the short list of people she trusted. She agreed with me that it made sense for her pastor to know about her therapy. No one person is indispensable to the therapy process. It is always good to involve safe, supportive people in a patient's recovery process.

Anger

I asked Dorothy about her anger. I frequently ask patients about their anger, even if it's not presented as a challenge. I believe the way we handle anger provides an insight into how we do our lives and thus how to do therapy. Anger can be repressed or dealt with openly. If it is not resolved in some way, it stockpiles. I soon found out that Dorothy did not express her anger openly. Not surprisingly, it erupted occasionally in overwhelmingly furious rages. I also wanted to hear about a life situation in which Dorothy was in touch with her anger.

Multiple Therapists

Referring Dorothy to other therapists for a few sessions allowed her to be exposed to a variety of techniques and personalities. Almost all of my patients see at least one other therapist. They are likely to be doing work with other therapists who have specific areas of expertise, such as couples communication, anger/forgiveness, codependency or compulsivity. The advantage of seeing several therapists is it decreases overdependence on one person, and two or three heads are always better than one. Dorothy would have the freedom to work with the therapist who made the most sense for her.

Hope

By the end of the first session, I wanted Dorothy to have some hope that doing therapy could make a difference in her life. Hope might be that for the first time she told someone else what was going on inside. Patients sometimes believe they are untreatable or terminally unique. When I was a patient in therapy, it was important to me to be heard by the therapist and to gain hope that the process would make a difference in my life. Something I said to Dorothy gave her hope: "You're not the first person I've seen with these kinds of challenges. My experience leads me to believe that we can get you to a better place." As Dorothy's first session came to a close, I wanted to let her know I would be available to her if she decided to work with me as her primary therapist.

2

The Match Game

—Dorothy—

Life went on while I did therapy. It meant one more activity and one more expense in my overcrowded, overspent life. My husband, John, and I have a daughter, Julie. In addition, I have two children, Celeste and Dan, from a previous marriage. Besides rearing a family, John and I worked together in marketing and sales. As a result, we spent time with many different people. Since we also connected with people at our church through music and drama activities, our "people plate" overflowed.

I liked people, but being with them drained me. Speaking in front of hundreds of people felt more comfortable than spending time with individuals. More and more I began to seek isolation. I rationalized this as the preference of a private person who needed time alone.

Overbooked, exhausted and afraid, I began the process of therapy, despite the fact that it required a time commitment I didn't think I had. And here I was, facing at least three more appointments before I saw Ralph again. The goal for my next appointment was to complete a genogram with one of the staff therapists. I understood this to be a drawing similar to a family tree with labels of attributes or characteristics attached to the people in the drawing. As I named the people in my family, the therapist questioned me about all of them and drew them schematically. What were they like? Did they have any addictions? Were they abusive, funny, smart, disabled . . . ?

I watched with fascination as my family was drawn out before my eyes. The questions came so fast I didn't have time to think about the answers. Feelings raced to the surface as patterns emerged. *I shouldn't be telling him these things. These are personal family things, and I'm supposed to keep them to myself. Stop talking!* I guess many of us were raised on that rule. But another thought arose as well. *You are safe. You may proceed.*

Questions raced through my mind. Who were the people I called family? What darkness did they spread? What light? Where did I fit? How did they see me? Could I remove the blinders and accept the reality of my experience? Did I contribute to the chaos?

I used to try to rationalize my family experience. *Well, any family story, told all at once, would sound crazy.* I told my family story in that session, and it did sound crazy: addictions to alcohol, sex and work. Uncontrolled and uncontrollable moods. Confusion, fear and abandonment. Frightened children and angry adults. Abuse that was verbal, emotional and physical. God at the center—impotent, removed, uncaring. Power struggles, silent cries in the night. Dysfunction, blame, generational secrets, lies. Family photo: smiling, controlled, vacant faces. Children grow, patterns continue. Divorce, affairs, rage. Pretense, denial, disillusionment. Hatred.

It also sounded like this: rainbow after the storm, embraces in the night, tears of remorse, gentle dreams. Surprises, smiles, encouragement, support. "You can do it." Artists, writers, tennis players. Trumpets, pianos. Reunion, renewal, brave new relationships. Community, transparency, new beginnings. God at the center—loving, strong, whole, powerful. Remarriage, reconciliation, children, creativity. Love.

At the end of the hour, the therapist told me that Ralph would evaluate the completed genogram during my next appointment. I began to enjoy becoming acquainted with different therapists and therapy techniques to determine which one suited me. I wasn't being pressured by anyone, and I would be the one to choose the therapist with whom I worked.

I had two more appointments to attend before my next session with Ralph. I was still nervous. At each appointment I completed homework and built a model of my life, using different techniques. Different therapists used their specialties to help create a collage of thoughts, feelings and experiences that added up to "Dorothy." What encouraged my self-disclosure? Each therapist supported and challenged me. Each was honest about what the therapist could do and about what only I could do.

At the next session I created a trauma egg. I drew an egg on a large sheet of art paper. Using crayons, colored pencils and pens, I drew lines representing every trauma that I could ever remember. No hurt was too small or too insignificant to list. It was my experience, and no one critiqued or questioned it. I labeled each trauma with a feeling that I had about it. Each label included a date. Around the egg I listed all the people I had ever trusted. All of them had passed away except for John, my friend Connie and my pastor.

As I drew the trauma egg, a certain memory came to mind. At an early age I made a conscious choice to be angry instead of frightened. I was about eight years old. It was as though I raised my fist and made a vow never to hurt again. I would be in control of my pain. No one would see me hurt, not even me. Even now I have to consciously give myself permission to feel hurt and to express sadness and fear. I no longer paper over my emotions with anger.

In another session I learned to journal about my day. I was able to express my feelings in prayers that I wrote out. Ralph recognized this early in the therapy process. Writing, especially writing prayers, allowed me to access feelings without censoring them. The therapists I worked with wanted to see samples of my writing. Allowing my words to be read felt much safer than saying them. When Ralph asked me to read my writing aloud, I sometimes said no. It was too scary. Sometimes he would read what I had written. That was scary too.

The quick pace helped move me into productive and focused therapy. The intensive assessment process gave me an opportunity to see the past and begin to determine how it affected my future.

I enjoyed the homework that therapy required, even though I approached it as if it were to be graded. I needed a quiet, safe place to work on it. This was "feeling stuff," and I couldn't get into it easily. Often I listened to soothing music as I struggled with a given assignment. It never occurred to me not to complete an assignment. Certain things I did compliantly. Homework was one of them.

After a month of assessment therapy it was time for me to choose my primary therapist. Each time I met with a new person, I mentally checked off a list of personal characteristics: female or male, introverted or extroverted, energetic or easygoing, nurturing or diffident. Did the therapist sit too close or too far away? Did the therapist hear what I said or hear what I meant? Was the therapist attentive or preoccupied? Did time pass quickly or did it drag on forever?

Like Goldilocks, I was seeking something that matched my needs. Which therapist seemed "just right" for me emotionally? In two sessions I almost cried. The porridge was too hot. In another session we both intellectualized the whole time. The porridge was too cold. In my session with Ralph the emotional energy seemed balanced. The porridge was just right. I decided to continue my work with Ralph and booked an appointment with him.

Therapy appointments had to be made well in advance. My first appointment was scheduled a week after I called. Subsequent appointments were not as easy to come by. Ralph's patient load kept him busy, and I often scheduled a month or two of appointments at a time. My appointments became part of my personal routine.

I was sitting in the waiting room again, longing for the safety of Ralph's office. "Hi, Dorothy. How are you?" called a voice from the hallway. I couldn't believe it! I had traveled to Scottsdale in the first place to obtain counseling without anyone knowing about it, and I ran into someone who knew me and wanted to carry on a conversation in front of a waiting room full of people. Ralph was running late, so I ran an even greater risk of being recognized by someone I knew. But I repressed the anger I felt and responded with a smile, "Hi, I'm fine. How are you?"

We chatted until Ralph showed up. "I hate to break this up, but would you please come back with me, Dorothy?" Great, now she knew that I was waiting to see Ralph instead of waiting for a friend or a family member. Oh well, I'd worry about that later.

Once in the office, I pursued my concern. "Ralph, don't you have a private entrance that I could use to avoid running into people I know?"

"Yes I have one and no you can't use it," he answered.

"Why not?" I persisted.

"Because I think that running into people you know helps you," he said. I was getting nowhere, so I waited for him to change the subject. "I see that you have completed a genogram and a trauma egg. You've spent time with three other therapists. Have you decided on one?" he asked.

I wanted to say that I would work with anyone who would let me come in the backdoor, but I didn't. "I'd like to work with you. I enjoyed the other sessions, but I trust you and I like your direct manner."

"Great! Let's meet every two weeks for a while and see how it goes. Now we can look over your genogram and your trauma egg, unless you have something else you want to discuss," he continued. He brought them out, and then we discussed relationships and my feelings about them. As we talked, I wondered why he was asking those particular questions. I was curious about the process that I was involved in.

Ralph helped me identify destructive patterns that I learned from my family and continued to follow. It's one thing to identify who is really to blame, but it's sobering to look at your own contribution to the cycle. Gently and deliberately we moved through my life.

My family did not make great relationship choices. I entered my first marriage when I was seventeen, pregnant and seemingly without options. The following nine years were difficult and sometimes traumatic. Anger, rage and fear pushed me, pulled me and enabled me to seek other destructive relationships. Those around me ignored my pain. Members of both of our extended families rationalized our problems and made excuses for them, even as they were caught in their own patterns of secrecy and fear. At seventeen I ran away from one dysfunctional family only to create another one. My two beautiful children were caught in a cycle they didn't create.

Ralph talked about ways to extinguish those behaviors, and we looked at new behaviors. For instance, he helped me begin to talk about my feelings with John and our children. I learned to set boundaries with people who were abusive toward me. I let go of anger and began to replace it with feelings that were more difficult to experience, like hurt and sadness.

Ralph's style of therapy was to listen, encourage, "carefront" (a word coined by David Augsburger which means to care about the person you are confronting) and actively interact. I didn't want someone who listened passively without offering feedback. I wanted someone who was as involved in the process of my therapy as I was. "Dorothy, it's time to go. Is there anything else you would like to bring up before we end today?"

I don't know how he did it. I never saw him look at his watch or glance at the clock on the end table next to me. Absorbed in our conversation, I was startled when he told me our time was up. Sometimes we talked for a full hour, and sometimes we ended at fifty minutes. A therapy hour actually meant something less than sixty minutes—not an easy concept for someone who tended to be literal.

The choice was made, the schedule was determined and the goals were set, providing the structure for the work Ralph and I had set out to accomplish. It is no small choice to decide to entrust someone with your life. Ralph seemed trustworthy.

—*Ralph's Notes*—

Dorothy's experience of feeling drained around people and her desire to isolate herself are symptoms of depression. Depression can be tiring and can result in low energy. Throughout therapy Dorothy resisted a diagnosis of depression, telling me that I was wrong. That ended the discussion in her mind.

I can't always read people's moods, not even my own. Dorothy had a tough time getting in touch with her own feelings, although she was pretty demonstrative nonverbally. Her eyes were expressive and her demeanor was vivacious when she was not depressed. When she was depressed, she lacked energy. Nevertheless, she managed to maintain her activities. Doing therapy while depressed meant participating partially, as opposed to being fully in the moment. Frequently her depression was masked by anger.

Impression Manager
Dorothy performed well, which explained her ability to speak comfortably in front of hundreds of people. However, she was always ready to escape from small groups or one-on-one situations. Dorothy didn't appear to be an anxiety-ridden person. Her presentation of self maximized the part of her that proclaimed, "I'm on top of the world, and that's all you'll ever see." But Dorothy's

confidence in the public arena belied her masked interior. It helped in therapy to remember her fragile side—the side that she concealed from the rest of the world.

Intimacy drained Dorothy. She feared opening up to others or to herself. She displayed tremendous resistance toward sharing her personal story with anyone. Her resoluteness in seeking therapy and in agreeing to see a variety of therapists initially spoke of Dorothy's determination to get through her fears.

Impression management comes from poor self-esteem: I don't think I'm really as good as I'm behaving. As Dorothy learned to like herself, she didn't worry nearly as much about the impressions she made on other people. It's tiring to control information, to defend oneself endlessly and to make sure certain secrets don't get out. For Dorothy that meant saying the right thing, being helpful to others, looking good, having right thoughts and presenting a favorable image.

A part of me is an impression manager. I can remember ridiculous examples of how important impressions were for me earlier in my career. I served a church in Winchester, Massachusetts, when I was attending Harvard Divinity School. On my day off once I saw a church member at a market where I shopped. Embarrassed because I was wearing something other than what I considered "correct pastoral attire," I tried to go down another aisle to avoid running into the person. Needless to say, my attempt to hide myself didn't work out.

Other Therapists

I frequently have a patient do some work with one or two other therapists before seeing me for a second appointment. I have other therapists do the genograms because they do them better. Insights from other therapists can be helpful both for the patient and for me. I appreciated Dorothy's willingness to cooperate in this, because she came in with fears about the therapy process. Dorothy's accepting my recommendation to work with other therapists represented a huge step toward establishing trust and stretching toward growth.

The Genogram

I asked Dorothy to do a genogram because I was interested in getting to know her through patterns in her family—for example, addictions, family interactions, divorce, death, similarities and differences, intimacy role models and parenting. Building a genogram identifies these areas and gives us access to them.

Dorothy knew a lot about her family. Some people don't. A lack of family information leads me to anticipate little awareness of family dynamics from the patient's perspective. Dorothy understood much more about family dynamics than most patients who come in for therapy. However, Dorothy feared talking about her family. Telling family secrets, even to a family therapist, is tough. Dorothy was well programmed to be a private person. Many patients adhere to a no-talk rule concerning family issues.

Dorothy's completed genogram revealed several patterns that she carried into her own life. As a youngster she had no intimacy role models. There were no words on her genogram that connoted emotional connection. Enormous deprivation showed up in the genogram. It is no wonder Dorothy tended to isolate at times.

Dorothy's marital history reflected patterns that she learned from her family. Dorothy's first marriage was dysfunctional and abusive. Married at the age of seventeen, Dorothy created her own intimacy-disabled family. The marriage ended in divorce, and Dorothy married a man unlike her first husband—a nice guy with passive-aggressive tendencies. Her second husband, John, was highly unlikely to be physically or emotionally abusive. But he was a scary partner for Dorothy because of his desire for closeness. Because he shared her very conservative religious background, Dorothy would have a hard time making a case for getting rid of him. The part of Dorothy that feared intimacy wanted to run away. Being connected to someone meant being controlled by someone.

It can be difficult to live with a nice guy because issues are seldom revealed in an overt way. John was a financial planner, and he hurt their relationship when he did not apply his financial expertise to his own life. Poor financial choices that he made put a tremendous strain on the marriage.

John and Dorothy participated in some joint sessions. I learned that John is not a detail person, whereas Dorothy is. John enjoys embellishing stories, whereas Dorothy likes fastidiously literal accounts. Each partner brought to the marriage entrenched, detrimental patterns.

Growing up, Dorothy was mentored to become intimacy disabled. She had a workaholic side. For a while anger was the only emotion Dorothy knew how to show. The relationships Dorothy chose were destined to keep her from emotional intimacy. People she wanted in her life were unavailable to her, while she herself was unavailable to those who wanted her. She was well established in avoidance patterns when she met John.

The Perfect Therapist

Dorothy's Goldilocks approach to selecting a therapist illustrates her need for perfection, including her perfectionistic expectations of her therapist. I remember several times in our therapy process where Dorothy's frustration about my "performance" led me to say, "Dorothy, if someone could be of more help to you, you can fire me at any time." This response triggered Dorothy's abandonment anxiety, and she responded with anger. This kind of incident has happened with other patients, and I have learned to be less abrupt when I state things that might trigger abandonment fears.

Working with an imperfect therapist helped Dorothy reexamine the expectations that she held for herself and John. Working through perfectionism led to tough times for Dorothy as she learned to be flexible and for me as I let go of my own need to meet those expectations.

There is a side of me that wants to do perfect therapy all the time. Having been a therapist for thirty years, I have reason to believe that I'm probably not going to do "perfect" therapy in this lifetime. Maybe God will ask me to be a therapist in heaven and will provide me with perfect ability to do it. But maybe no one in heaven will need therapy!

Components of the Therapeutic Process

Homework is a big part of therapy and keeps the work going between sessions. Some people resist homework. In that case homework becomes a therapeutic issue. My own style is to make it clear that patients are wasting my time, as well as their own time (and money), if they don't do homework. We then talk about whether therapy makes sense for them. Dorothy was the ideal patient in the area of homework. She did everything I asked her to do, and sometimes she did more. Homework gave her an opportunity to speed up the therapy process and to reflect on her feelings and thoughts between sessions.

Dorothy's second experience with other therapists was with a female therapist who was certified in art therapy. Together they drew a trauma egg that depicted all of the negative or traumatic events of Dorothy's life. That process offered Dorothy another modality to use in gaining understanding about herself. Dorothy's egg showed that her impressions of her family of origin were balanced, including parts that she valued and parts that were painful.

Dorothy's memory for details was obvious. Her organizational abilities jumped out from the trauma egg in the detailed chronological listing of traumatic events occurring throughout her life. Dorothy's egg, combined with her genogram, certainly validated the importance of getting family information at the beginning of the counseling process. I went through the trauma egg with her on at least three occasions. We also reviewed John's trauma egg and Dorothy's trauma egg together.

Early in her trauma egg exercises Dorothy dealt with experiences of being scared or of being accused of something she didn't do. During her growing-up years she was subjected to unpredictable mood swings and rigid rules. She depicted some later events with heavy black lines lacking descriptive terms or dates. Those traumas were extremely difficult for Dorothy to talk about. She brought them out in the open much later with a great deal of hesitancy. The egg provided a clue to areas she deeply wanted to work through but feared verbalizing. Getting in touch with her pain helped Dorothy move through what was troubling her in the present. We did not review every bit of trauma but focused on major issues.

Choosing a Primary Therapist

A good match between therapist and client significantly enhances the progress of therapy. A patient who really wants to make changes (as Dorothy did) needs to work at finding the right match in a therapist. Over the years some patients have experienced me as too confrontational, while others have found me not confrontational enough. Some patients think I want to deal with feelings too much of the time, and others want to spend more time in experiential therapy. The reasons behind these varying preferences are not always clear.

It would be ludicrous for me to say that I'm always the same person or that I approach all patients in the same way. Outside events can affect the patient and the therapist. At times I can be abrupt and not as focused as I should be, even though I work hard to remain intent on the process. If that is the case, I may not hear what the patient is trying to tell me.

When Dorothy and I went through the genogram and trauma egg initially, I wanted to help Dorothy reach a decision about who would make the most sense as her primary therapist. Sometimes patients think I'm trying to get rid of them, so I need to handle this matter delicately. If patients respond to this with feelings of abandonment, I explain the process carefully. Very few people have flatly refused to see other therapists in the course of their therapy.

Safe Exit

Dorothy freely shared her feelings about issues such as my being late, her wanting to leave through a back exit or anything else that was uncomfortable for her. But when it came to deeper feelings about issues that affected her life, it was more difficult for her to express her emotions.

Dorothy wanted to leave through a back exit to avoid being seen by people she knew. We do have a back entrance that is used by therapists and office people. It is not used by patients most of the time. A few patients incur such pain in therapy that they want to get out of the building as quickly as possible. For them exceptions have been made. Occasionally we do custody evaluations, and it may be appropriate for the parents to leave by separate exits. But our policy is to encourage patients to learn that nothing calamitous happens when they encounter an acquaintance in the waiting room.

Goal Setting

Destructive family patterns do get passed from one generation to the next. Dorothy's frustration and anger at some of the destructive features in her own family led her to "medicate" her feelings by doing destructive things herself. Dorothy had the intelligence and the understanding to make smart choices, but she was not able to express love or anger. Consequently, she looked for validation and love in "all the wrong places."

Dorothy cared deeply about the emotional and spiritual growth of her children Dan and Celeste, even though she had made decisions that were destructive to herself and to them. Julie, however, has grown up in a very different environment and appears to enjoy life a great deal. I had the opportunity to see Celeste three or four times. Her mom's improved marital situation seems to be good for her. She has seen that relationships can improve and that it makes sense to do therapy. Celeste is learning a lot from her mom. They have a close, sometimes sisterly relationship that is fun for them. At the same time, Dorothy remains the mother in that relationship.

Celeste clearly respects her stepfather, John, and knows him to be a nice guy whom she can trust to help. I have no direct knowledge of Julie or Dan, although I've been around Julie enough to observe the fun side of her. Julie is a real helper to others.

The sins of one generation don't have to be passed on to the next generation. Dorothy broke the cycle of rejecting and fearing intimacy. Currently she is tremendously more "intimacy able" than her parents were when she was growing up and much more comfortable with intimacy than she was four or five years ago. Dorothy demonstrates that dramatic changes are possible when a person mobilizes personal resources, effective therapy and a strong belief in God.

3

Healing Moments
—Dorothy—

"Close your eyes, relax, and tell me what happened next," Ralph instructed.

"I'm in a cold, crowded waiting room. I'm alone, numb and sick. It's like I'm in the room but not in it. Away from the noise and the people."

"Tell me more of what you see and what you are feeling," Ralph said in a soft voice that sounded like somebody else's. I thought about screaming, *Quit being gentle and kind. I don't deserve your kindness. Be direct and confrontive with me. I can't handle your empathy. Stop it!* Instead I said, "I see lots of people. Patients, family members, nurses. I'm terrified and I feel very small. I want to disappear."

"What happened to you next?" he continued.

"I don't know. There's another room. I'm on a table and everyone is ignoring me. I'm scared and I'm sick, but they talk over me like I'm not a person. When I'm scared, I disconnect from what's going on, so I try to do that. But the lights are too bright. I can't leave. I've had some kind of medication, and I can't move."

"Can you tell me more?" he prompted.

"I think so. I can't remember much. Someone is coming toward me with something metal in his hands. They think I'm asleep, but I'm not. I want to yell at them to put me out, but I can't. That's all I remember." That's as far as I'll go with Ralph. I felt a tremendous need to leave, but I stayed. "I don't want to talk about this anymore," I stated emphatically. "What I did was wrong and I knew it."

"You were sixteen years old, and there was a tremendous amount of pain going on in your life," Ralph said.

"I knew having an abortion was wrong."

"Dorothy, don't you think God has forgiven you?"

"Yes. No. I don't know. It was wrong, and I knew it. God has probably forgiven me, but I can't forgive myself." I was confused and he was confusing me more. I wanted this hour to be over. I wanted to leave. Why didn't I just get up and walk out?

Ralph sat back in his chair and was quiet for a moment. He seemed to be thinking about what to do next. Finally, he leaned forward and said, "Dorothy, I want you to write a prayer to God about the two abortions you had when you were a teenager and bring it in with you the next time we meet. Is that OK?"

"Fine," I replied. Lately he had asked me to write prayers to God about everything. It did seem to help when I couldn't verbalize something on an emotional level. This time I was agitated by his request, which I didn't think would help. But I probably would have agreed to anything at that point just to get out of there. We switched to another topic for the rest of the hour. When it was time to leave, I bolted out the door, thinking I probably wouldn't come back.

When I returned for my next appointment, I had my prayer in hand.

"Dorothy, would you read your prayer out loud?" Ralph asked.

"If that is a question and I have an option, then the answer is no." I didn't like reading my prayers out loud—too personal.

"I have to be very careful how I phrase things with you. Dorothy, please read your prayer for me. How's that?" he added with a smile.

With a quick glare I began to read.

Psalm 139:13-14, 16 says,

For you created my inmost being;
    you knit me together in my mother's womb.
I praise you because I am fearfully
    and wonderfully made; . . .
    your eyes saw my unformed body.
All the days ordained for me
    were written in your book
    before one of them came to be.

Dear God,

I am praying about the abortions I had. "All the days ordained for me." But no days were ordained for them—my children. I should have protected them. That's what mothers do for their children. But they needed to be protected *from* me. I'm willing to talk to you about this; please help me express my feelings. I've kept this from you—not how it happened but how I felt about it. Show me how to forgive myself and those who were part of it. I knew it was wrong, but I didn't think about it. I wanted relief from the pain. The pain truly was intolerable. And I didn't know you were there to help me.

I'd give anything to do it over. I'm stronger now. You are my strength. My heart is crushed, and I'm unable to get away from the pain. That's why I'm working toward the pain. Please help me work through it.

Show me how to forgive myself. Thank you for prompting me to talk to Ralph about it. It wasn't so much what he said but the intensity of his words that made an impact on me. He felt so strongly that I wasn't letting myself off the hook and that I should. He said it was very clear. It startled me because I told him I knew at the time it was wrong, and he still felt I could forgive myself.

How it must grieve you! We don't forgive ourselves when you have forgiven us. I want to grieve for those babies. I miss them. Can I find a place in my heart for them that isn't filled with contempt for what I did? I need your forgiveness and more; I need your healing.

Why didn't anyone give me viable options? Couldn't anyone see the torment I was in? Once the decisions were made, I acted like a zombie. I remember nothing about the second time and very little about the first time. I was so sick. The airplane trip to the city and then the van ride to the hospital were awful. Everyone in the group laughed and joked while I was alone. It was a surreal field trip of participants who were no longer individuals and were acting as if this were an everyday event. Blood tests, paperwork, waiting, those awful hospital gowns. Then going into the surgery room where nurses and doctors were joking. I was still awake, but I couldn't talk. I wanted to scream at them to put me out.

My motive wasn't to be rid of those babies; I wanted to stop the incredible pain.

Thank you for reminding me of the past. You are helping me to forgive myself. When I think of those two children, I think of them with you, playing, laughing and being loved so dearly. I am their mom, and I love them. I never thanked you for their lives, Lord. I want to do that. Thank you for the gift of their life. I didn't know it at the time, but it was a gift just the same. No one can rob me of that anymore. Much was robbed of me, and I robbed myself of even more.

If you want me to remember more of my time with those two precious souls, then I embrace that journey. I will no longer place myself in condemnation over this. I will think of my children whenever I need to, and I will grieve for them.

You've given me back something from this loss. Ralph said to let God be God. Help me to do that.

I love you,

Dorothy

In the novel *Alice's Adventures in Wonderland* the Cheshire Cat "vanished quite slowly, beginning with the end of the tail, and ending with the grin, which remained some time after the rest of it had gone." Those words also describe the process I had experienced of losing who I was created to be. I began to disappear as a result of the pain of living. Little by little I vanished until the only recognizable thing about me was the grin I presented to the world.

I don't know why therapy works, but it does. My three years in therapy included many times of healing. Some of them had to do with my past relationships. Others had to do with my present beliefs about life and how they interfere with current relationships. Ralph and I didn't spend an enormous amount of time on my past, but I did look at it enough to understand why I behaved in a reactionary way in some situations and isolated myself in others. Looking back helped me gain access to my feelings because I had turned them off at such a young age. The feeling I felt most comfortable with was anger. It was useful in protecting myself from being overwhelmed by other emotions.

Looking back was difficult for me but yielded insights. I looked to free myself, although I indulged in some blaming. It felt good, and Ralph seemed to know how much was healthy for me to experience.

During another time of healing I wrote a prayer about the looking-back process. I resisted revisiting a time in my life when I made some poor decisions about relationships. So guess what Ralph had me do? Write a prayer about it. My letters to God usually were written with a specific verse of Scripture in mind.

"Let us go back to Judea." (John 11:7)

Dear God,

"Let us go back to Judea." What are you thinking? The

thought of that scares me. To go back to a place in my life where I was all but crushed? To journey back to that time when everything in me cries out to stay away from it? And so I answer, "You want me to go back there?"

Just as the disciples were startled by the suggestion to go back to Judea, a place where you had been hurt in the past, so am I. My Judea places seem best forgotten, avoided, denied. Even the suggestion that I go back paralyzes me with fear.

I've structured everything I do to avoid those places. Anything that comes close to those experiences I try to avoid. Feelings, thoughts, memories and relationships related to those experiences must be denied.

If I run into people from my Judea, I want to hide. My fear of the past reaches into my present experience. Either I distrust people because I believe they will harm me or I fear their distrust of me.

Judea controls me. But if I go back, under your protection, and look at it, I can gain an understanding of the dynamics and truth about that particular place in my life. I see where I was frightened and where I frightened others. Sometimes in my fear of being overpowered I fought back and hurt others and myself. I was reactionary and lived to survive. When I go back, I can learn to accept the harm I caused. There may still be things that trigger old responses, but you can teach me to respond differently.

It is a journey worth taking because looking at my past with you takes away the fear. While I can never, not even for one moment, change my past, I can embrace the healing you offer in my present.

You amaze me. How gentle you are in my recovery and in my life. You never insist on my taking any step toward healing. I am so confident in your timing.

Love,
Dorothy

Healing moments in therapy also helped me heal physically. I love to run, walk and climb mountains. I hate stretching and loosening up. I love doing everything I can in life as fast as I can. I hate sitting and doing nothing. I love doing things while I'm doing things. You know, reading while brushing my teeth, ironing while talking on the phone, doing homework while watching TV, updating my day planner while sitting at a red light, learning my lines in a play while having my teeth worked on.

One particularly hectic Christmas during my second year in therapy, my back decided to spasm while I was "doing things." It hurt, but if I moved just right I could still keep doing what I was doing. So I continued to act in the Christmas play at our church, taking massive doses of muscle relaxants and crawling off stage between lines.

One night I felt a fiery hot blade cutting down through my back and leg. The slightest movement caused excruciating pain. Somehow I got to the emergency room, where I was x-rayed and given Demerol. Nothing showed up on the films. Three doctors and an expensive MRI could find no physical reason for my distress.

Two things helped my recovery. First, a wonderful neurosurgeon explained back injuries to me and showed me my x-rays. He said I had a very healthy spine but some swelling that could be pressing on a nerve. We talked about healthy ways to exercise and stretch to increase my flexibility and keep my back functioning as it should.

Second, there was Ralph. Later that week I stood looking out the window as I waited for him to take me to his office. "Looking out the window," he commented when he came for me. "Come on back to my office, please. What's going on? I noticed you were staring out the window."

Ralph was very good at noticing nonverbal cues from me. My nonverbal communication often spoke volumes about what I was feeling or experiencing. "I'm having back pain, and your waiting-room seats are horribly uncomfortable. These chairs in your office aren't much better, so excuse me if I stand up."

"I'm really sorry about your back. What are you doing for it?" he asked. I explained to him the whole drama surrounding my injury and waited for more sympathy. "Dorothy, what do you do to relax?"

"Relax?" I shouted. "What does relaxing have to do with anything? I'm in serious pain, and you're talking about relaxing?"

"I'd really like you to look at some ways to relax that might help your physical symptoms. I think learning to unwind and staying centered would be very helpful to you."

It was amazing the things he would come up with. I started to think about all the ways I didn't relax throughout the day. I spent a lot of time feeling tired and tense. And so began my interest in relaxation techniques.

I'm still not great at relaxing, but I've come a long way and my back pain has disappeared. I recognize when I'm getting out of balance emotionally, physically or spiritually. My body doesn't have to react with headaches, back pain or illness to get my attention. I'm not saying all physical illness is a result of emotional stress, but for me they do seem to be connected.

I don't usually experience depression—I'm just too busy to be down. Being bedridden by pain gave me an opportunity to experience feelings I didn't often pay attention to. During my recuperation I gave myself some homework. I wrote a letter to God based on Jeremiah 38:12, which says, "Put these old rags and worn-out clothes under your arms to pad the ropes."

Dear God,

How like you to give us "old rags and worn-out clothes" to pad us as we are being helped and protected. Jeremiah was being rescued from a deep well. You sent him people to rescue him and ropes to pull him to safety. But most of all you gave him "old rags and worn-out clothes."

You deeply care that I might be injured or hurt even as I am pulled to freedom. The process of being restored is painful. You send me the padding that cushions me along the way.

How I long for and cherish the ways in which you cushion my life as I am pulled out of the deep cisterns. The places where I would most certainly die spiritually, emotionally and physically.

The cistern places of my life are perilous, but the climb out is dangerous too. I must rely on people you've sent to rescue me or to aid me in the rescue. The rescue will not even begin if I don't accept their help. I need to reach out and grab the rope.

I, for my part, must grab hold and choose to live. Choose to be restored even though life will not be easy outside the well. My nights and alone times feel like the inside of a well. Dark and closed in, trapped and alone. There seems to be no way out.

Then you send people to help me. You give me so many who throw down rope. It's interesting that in my weakened state I do little of the work. Other people help when I'm at the bottom. I just need to hold on tight. I need to trust them to not let go. There it is again—trust in people! That's my part.

Finally, I'm surrounded by the padding that cushions the rescue. Your Spirit is the padding that protects and encases my fragility. I am vulnerable even though I'm perceived as being strong. There are many areas in which I'm very fragile.

Thank you for the rescue team. I love the people in my life who care for me as family. What a gift! And I love you and your unfailing protection. Your constant cushion of love surrounds me, just as the "old rags and worn-out clothes" cushioned Jeremiah.

I adore you,
Dorothy

—Ralph's Notes—

Dorothy shared the painful story of her two abortions. Walking through her memories with her was tough. I remembered what I was like as a teenager and was struck by the immensity of what being pregnant meant for sixteen-year-old Dorothy.

Listening is key to a therapist, as it is to all relationships. To listen is not to preach, shame, condone or condemn. Jesus was the ultimate listener. When therapists do counseling from their own biases, destructive contamination can occur. An example of this would be when a Christian counselor gets on his or her high horse and begins to preach and not do counseling—that is, dealing with the value system of the patient in a constructive way. All therapists have biases. But it is important not to let biases get in the way of being there in a healing way for patients.

My goal in helping Dorothy work through her abortions was to join her in the journey. When I have ears to hear what another person is trying to say, I become less rigid in my own point of view. I can maintain my own beliefs even as I listen to others.

The choice Dorothy faced as a teenager had to be made very quickly and had to be made amid fear and blinding pain. That same situation could have been a teachable moment if the right resources had been available.

I'm not naive enough to think that even a young person in the most ideal family is likely to turn to family or church in a crisis; that is likely to happen only when there is open communication and unconditional love. Overcontrol frequently leads to under that control of the person who feels manipulated. I always try to help patients be true to themselves and to their understanding of God's will for their lives.

Isolation

Patients experience isolation at many levels. A person who suffers a crisis or trauma can become catatonic and withdraw. Dorothy did not become catatonic, but she did isolate from God and self in many ways. Instead of being in charge of her life as a feeling adult, she suffered a kind of posttraumatic stress disorder. She didn't dissociate entirely, yet she lost a large period of her life in terms of being in charge of her experience and being connected to God and to others.

Dorothy was not able to tell her story. She did not feel forgiven, and she viewed her actions as if they added up to the unpardonable sin. Dorothy's isolation led her to something of a split. Part of her knew Scripture, went to church and was highly organized and accomplished. The other part acted out in ways that were destructive and hurtful to herself and to others. Trying to be connected to someone while avoiding pain led to relationships that were destined to fail, including her first marriage. Intimacy meant hurt and suffering to Dorothy, and she did everything she could to stay out of the pain. Integration of her spiritual and emotional sides occurred only with therapy.

Spiritual Issues

Therapists cannot deal with a patient's spirituality or sexuality unless they have dealt with their own issues. It doesn't make sense to enter into a therapeutic relationship in areas where the therapist has hang-ups. Anyone who has failed to examine her or his beliefs to see if they make sense from a grown-up perspective probably has "borrowed beliefs," ideas that have been borrowed from others such as parents or teachers.

It is an important spiritual moment to move from a belief system that was taught to a belief system that is owned internally. It is freeing to be able to state one's beliefs clearly. This internal affirmation is therapeutic and stems neither from compliance nor from rebellion.

Every patient has faith issues. Each patient determines whether or not a spiritual issue is important enough to be addressed. If the patient says it isn't, then that is where it stays. Faith is like a fingerprint. No one has exactly the same faith or the same faith issues. Faith is not static; it changes and evolves.

Spirituality is not irrelevant in therapy. I prefer to work with a patient's spiritual adviser when it makes sense to do so. Accessing the other support systems in a patient's life can be helpful when they are healthy.

Remembering

As Dorothy worked through her own internal journey, I was careful to neither take away from nor add to her experience. It was important to avoid suggesting information that would contaminate her present-day experience. Therapists are privileged to share their patients' private moments. I think it's a form of intimacy that most people never share with anyone.

I believe it is the therapist's responsibility to help the patient share at a deep level with significant others. With Dorothy that meant learning to share those types of experiences and feelings with John and her family.

One of my goals was to facilitate Dorothy's opening up to herself. It was important to provide a safe place and a context to help her keep talking and not revert to the silence she was used to. Over the years I have used techniques such as hypnosis, image therapy and journaling to help patients remember experiences.

There are a number of paths that lead to the same place. But the therapist never suggests data that was not there.

I believe that Dorothy would reject any information that did not come from inside her. She rightfully and helpfully negated anything that was not congruent with her own belief system or experience. Sometimes I met resistance from Dorothy when I was on target. When I was off, I met even more. I almost always tell patients that it is part of the therapy contract to use their heads and to let me know when they disagree with what I have to say. That frees up the therapy process for both of us.

The goal of Dorothy's journey was knowledge of herself and clarification of her experience. My job as her coach was to work with her in a team relationship, to help her stay on that journey and to clarify what she already knew, to help her walk through areas that were frightening and painful, such as family-of-origin experiences.

If I'd Been There ...

Dorothy asked me what I would have done to help her if she had talked to me when she was a pregnant teenager. As a therapist, I help people make hard decisions. I would have helped Dorothy be honest with herself and with God. I would have asked her to pray about the decision she needed to make and would have had her consult with someone it made sense to talk to.

I have no idea what she would have done if more resources would have been available to her. It was unfortunate that Dorothy didn't know (and I believe many women do not know) someone who could help her work through her issues. The decision probably would have become one that was thoughtful, prayerful and spiritual. The moment could have been one of personal growth, accountability and maturation as opposed to isolation, fear and shame.

Why Therapy Works

Dorothy once commented, "I don't know why therapy works, but it does." I know the component parts that make it work for me and for others. The right moment or propitious time is also important. The teachable moment works best when the receiver of therapy has an open heart and mind.

Sometimes it works because I make commonsense points such as not maintaining a double standard for self and others. There is a theory that the things that most disturb us about others frequently represent a part of ourselves that we want to disown. When we are angry at people for being rigid and controlling, perhaps we are also angry at the part of ourselves that operates in the same way.

Looking Back to Look Forward

Sometimes talking through the past takes more time than it took for Dorothy. In the case of severe sexual, physical or emotional abuse, therapy may require spending time on the past while strengthening the present. It's especially helpful to share the shameful parts of the past with a safe person.

Talking or writing about events in her life that she had kept secret empowered Dorothy to let go of some of the fear tied to those events. Her past isolation and secretiveness reinforced her shame-based personality. She found it helpful to talk to another human being as well as God.

Painful Stress

I am frequently amazed at the link between physical symptoms and stress. I was not surprised when Dorothy experienced physical pain from the stress of how she did life. Dorothy found relief as she began to explore types of relaxation that made sense for her life.

Doing therapy can produce stress and working through tough issues can increase anxiety. It's important for patients to understand the process and to prepare for ways to relax and switch gears. Since Dorothy was so good at projecting a calm exterior, she kept her stress and tension concealed from both of us.

People find relief from stress in many different ways. Dorothy enjoys computers, reading, traveling and going on personal retreats away from everyone. I enjoy reading, traveling, sports, being with friends and family and exercising.

Self-Study

Dorothy gave herself homework during her recuperation period, which was part of the transition to taking care of herself and becoming less dependent on me. I'm always looking for ways to encourage patients to rely less on me and more on their own efforts to heal. Reading, talking to others, writing and introspection were some of the ways Dorothy took charge of her own recovery.

Old Rags and Worn-Out Clothes

I love the prayer Dorothy wrote about the process of being pulled to safety using "old rags and worn-out clothes." Dorothy comes across as a very strong person. She has numerous gifts. She's intelligent and fun, she has a quick sense of humor and her reactions are spontaneous. Because of those attributes, she appears to be a strong person, which is both a blessing and a curse.

The blessing comes from the fact that those abilities are there to be used in her life. The curse is that most people think Dorothy is always strong. If she doesn't choose to open up to someone and say she's scared, vulnerable, hurt or terrified, most people do not know what is going on with her. It's important for a person who appears so strong to do the really courageous thing and say, "Hey, I'm scared!"

Dorothy can intimidate some people. They find it very difficult to believe that inside her is a human being with the same kinds of fears they may have. "When I am weak, then I am strong" (2 Corinthians 12:10) truly illustrates the paradox of being vulnerable, transparent and strong. Dorothy's dramatic moments of therapy offered times of healing and growth.

4

Family, Ralph & Couples Therapy
—Dorothy—

Let's go to Grace Community Church today. They're having a guest speaker I want to hear. It'll be fun." It was Father's Day, and our entire family—John, me, Celeste (our twenty-year-old daughter), Dan (our seventeen-year-old son) and Julie (our eight-year-old daughter)—were celebrating it together. We were going to church and then eating out afterward. I had a special reason for us to attend a church other than our own.

"Why can't we go to our own church?" "Who's this speaker anyway?" "I want to go to my Sunday-school class, not listen to a boring speaker." What a response to my suggestion!

"Since it's Father's Day, a father and son who are psychologists here in the valley are having a dialogue. I think it will be interesting," I countered. "Besides, John wants to go there, and it's his choice today." I was using any ploy I could to get what I wanted.

We arrived at the church and sat together in the front row. When we took our seats, I looked down the row and saw Ralph and his family sitting there. This was frustrating. I wanted my family to see him, but I didn't want him to see my family. I hadn't told anyone yet about being in therapy except John, my pastor and my friend Connie. This was my way of easing into a conversation about my therapy, since Ralph and his son, Marcus, were the guest speakers that morning.

Ralph and Marcus introduced their presentation and began to speak to each other. It was interesting to see a father and son share about themselves before a large audience, just as if they were alone together at home. They were modeling good communication, and it looked so easy, so natural. I was fascinated.

After the service ended, I decided it was time for my family to meet Ralph, so I sent John over to say hi. He's an extrovert, and it's easy for me to hide behind him. As they were chatting together, I decided that it was safe to introduce the rest of the family. "Ralph, I'd like you to meet Celeste, Dan and Julie," John said. They all shook hands.

"I really enjoyed your presentation with your son, Ralph. Thank you for sharing," I said. I extended my hand to shake his. He paused, shook my hand and said, "Hi, Dorothy. It's good to see you."

Celeste was not about to let that pass. "So, how do you know my mom?" she asked. I was speechless and so was Ralph. Finally I choked out, "He spoke at a seminar I attended." Truthful to an extent.

"Yeah, but how do you know each other?" she persisted.

Then Ralph and I started talking at the same time, saying opposite things. It was an awkward moment, but I began the process of coming out of the closet about my therapy sessions. It was four months into therapy before I was able to tell the people closest to me that I spent an hour a week with someone talking through my life. Ralph had been encouraging me to tell my family, and I had been consistently adamant about not telling them. Intimate sharing wasn't something I was accustomed to, not even with the people I cared for the most.

The three children were pretty blasé in the face of my revelation. They asked me how much it cost and when I went. I finally realized that I needed to give them permission to ask me questions. Just as Ralph modeled communication for his audience, I had to model it for my family. I had modeled the no-talk rule for them to this point, and it would take time for them to become comfortable with opening up and sharing.

"It seems you opened a door for your family to know about your therapy sessions," Ralph said the next day in session.

"Yes, and I'm glad I did. After the service we went to dinner and I mentioned that I was going to therapy and that you are my therapist. Thank you again for sharing with others, as you did in the church service."

"Dorothy, I think it's time for John to come in with you for a session," Ralph said.

I thought, *Wow, that came out of the blue. Why does John need to come in? This is my time, and I don't want to share it with anyone. Besides, if he came in, I'm sure I'd be blamed for something. Being so easygoing, he always comes across as the good guy. Our marriage is fine. Why does Ralph want him to come in?* But all I said was "I don't think that's a good idea."

"OK, would you just tell John that I'd like to see you both even if you decide not to?"

"Yes, I can do that much," I answered. I knew I had the final say in regard to anything we talked about or any treatment we tried, but Ralph had a way of getting me to try something I normally would not do. He knew more about the techniques of therapy than I did, and I was convinced that he would not hurt me. It had taken me a long while to arrive at that level of trust, but it was important for our working relationship. In general, I tended not to trust people. Ralph knew this. And while he pushed for me to go forward, he understood my resistance.

Four months into therapy I was again seated in the waiting room, this time next to John. He seemed relaxed and chatted with the other people sitting there. He probably would have enjoyed running into someone he knew, for company.

"Hi John, hi Dorothy," came a familiar voice. I was beginning to think Ralph planted people in the waiting room just to desensitize me.

"Hi," came John's eager reply. Before I could bury myself in a magazine, he was chatting away like a tourist in an airport looking forward to a vacation trip. Ralph was late again and thus left us open to being spotted by people who were emerging from their therapy sessions into the waiting room. Now they would think that my marriage was in trouble too.

The first person to come around the corner was someone else we knew. Unbelievable! Again, John was conversing animatedly, and I was dying inside. Where was Ralph? Why was he always late?

"John, nice to see you again," Ralph said as he shook his hand. "Hello, Dorothy. Would you both please come to my office?" The routine began.

"Dorothy's freaking out because she keeps running into people she knows," John proclaimed.

"I know. She keeps trying to get permission to use a backdoor, but I won't let her." Ralph and John laughed together, and I glared at them both. This was not starting out the way I wanted. We chatted together for a few minutes and then Ralph said, "Dorothy, I'd like to have some time alone with John. Would you please wait in the other room until I call you?"

Fine with me, I thought. I wasn't enjoying this session much anyway. I still didn't understand why we both had to be there, and John talked too slowly. I liked rapid talk, fast-paced exchange, focus on me. I was feeling jealous of my time with Ralph. I was afraid that John would deflect Ralph's attention away from me. I sat in the waiting room feeling self-pity and loneliness.

Thirty minutes later Ralph came out to get me. He smiled, and as I passed him he said to me, "You are courageous and sensitive." He was an encourager, and I quit feeling like a jerk for being self-absorbed. After all, what was therapy about if not to focus on yourself for a while?

As soon as I entered the office, I could see that John had already shown me up. He had tears in his eyes. Before I could catch myself I blurted out, "Great, you cried, didn't you? I can't believe you're barely here and already you are emoting." I knew I sounded like a two-year-old, but sometimes I couldn't believe how emotional he was. This time he was crying because his dad had cancer.

"I'd like each of you to tell the other three things you like about that person," Ralph instructed. "Who wants to go first?"

"I will." I wasn't going to be outdone this time. This was easy. "John is sensitive, he's fun to be with and he's a great father." I meant what I said.

"OK, John, please tell me three things you like about Dorothy," Ralph continued.

John looked directly at me and said, "She's very intelligent, adventurous, organized, spontaneous, fun to be with, a great wife and mother," he ended.

Ralph asked for three things, not an endless list, I thought to myself. I was starting to feel annoyed by the tack Ralph was taking this time. John and I sat in the two swivel chairs. The creaking noise that John's chair was making was also annoying. I pushed my foot up against it to stop the noise. "Dorothy, why are you pushing your foot against John's chair?" Ralph interrupted.

To avoid answering his question, I replied, "I don't know."

"What do you mean you don't know? You know the answer to everything else I ask you in here." Ralph leaned forward in his chair and demanded an answer. I honestly didn't know the answer, but I had succeeded in getting Ralph's attention back on me. We pursued my agitation for a while, and then the session was over. "I'd like to continue seeing the two of you for a while," he ended.

"But I want to continue working on my own stuff," I said. *Good job, Dorothy. You spoke up for yourself and the world didn't come to an end.*

"OK, how about if I see you alone every other session?" Ralph offered. Our first session ended and we moved into the hallway.

"Hi, Dorothy. How are you?" John and Ralph broke into laughter as I ran into yet another person I knew.

By now I was on a roll, so I decided to tell other family members that I was in therapy. I started with my younger sister, Barbi. She had accompanied me to the seminar where we first saw Ralph.

I arranged to meet her for tea at the Ritz Hotel, a lovely setting where we could talk without being interrupted. At that time I believed that everyone saw me as the together person in the family. At least I thought that about myself. I could handle anything, and I achieved what I set out to do. I saw therapy as a sign of weakness and thought others would think the same thing.

After we had chatted for a while I said, "Remember that seminar we went to at church? Remember the author and psychologist who spoke? I'm seeing him once a week."

"I've been wondering when you were going to tell me," she answered.

"How did you know I was seeing him?" I asked.

"Some time ago I called to see if you could go somewhere with me on a Monday morning. Julie answered the phone and said you couldn't do anything on Monday because you go to Ralph's. I asked her who Ralph was and what the two of you did. Julie said, 'They don't do anything, they just sit and talk.'"

I wondered if everyone knew my "secret." Gradually I opened up to different people in my life about therapy. They had lots of questions about the process and my need for it. As I talked about my own journey, people opened up to me about theirs. This intimacy stuff was fun and energizing, unlike the drain I felt when I protected myself from others. I knew I was on to something.

—*Ralph's Notes*—

Every day people engage in many different kinds of conversations. Conversation can promote or discourage intimacy. The purpose of the father-son dialogue that my son Marcus and I presented was to model a form of communication that leads to a deepening intimacy. Father's Day seemed an appropriate time to challenge the worshipers gathered at Grace Community Church to look at their own style of communicating.

What I love about that particular kind of presentation is that it is unplanned and unrehearsed. Marcus is free to bring up whatever is on his mind, and so am I. The audience is aware of the format and is intrigued by the risk-taking involved. At least that is what people tell us when we finish our presentation.

I have had to work hard with my family to become comfortable with "hearing" whatever the speaker wants to say. It does not come naturally for me to listen without responding. It does not come naturally for Marcus to express his thoughts and feelings to me either. The audience, including Dorothy's family, witnessed a conversation that was unrehearsed, but we have spent a lot of time working through communication issues.

Audience

Dorothy, John and their children were sitting near my family. I enjoy recognizing people in the audience when I'm about to speak. I almost always encounter someone I know when I speak locally because I have lived and worked in the same community for nearly thirty years.

When a current or former patient is in the audience, I usually wait to be approached to say hello. I try very hard to honor patients who desire anonymity. Other patients may know me in a setting outside of the therapy office.

Dorothy had not told me she would be coming to Grace to hear me speak. I enjoyed the opportunity to meet John and the children. John greeted me first. I knew by now that Dorothy could test the waters relationally through others. I learned that John felt comfortable approaching just about anyone to say hi.

Celeste reacted when I greeted Dorothy. She wanted to know how I knew her mother and pushed for an answer that made sense to her. Dorothy took the lead in explaining our relationship. I understood from her answer that Dorothy's family did not know she was in therapy.

Couples Therapy

Asking John to join Dorothy and me for therapy triggered another reaction in Dorothy. Early in therapy, I did not have immediate access to her reactions. She could be absolutely churning inside but would not betray it externally. Once I became aware of the subtle shifts in nonverbal cues, such as tone of voice, I could better detect the truth behind her projected response.

Dorothy did not think that having John come in for couples therapy was a good idea. It is always helpful to have information from people who share the patient's living environment. Because Dorothy was married, I wanted to hear her spouse's view of her.

Dorothy did not bring any marriage issues to work on. In fact, she said her marriage was very good. John appeared on her trauma egg as a trusted person. That is certainly not the case in all marriages. I'm just as interested in hearing from the spouses of "perfect marriages" as I am from the spouses of troubled ones.

Waiting-Room Stress

Dorothy continued to feel stressed about the possibility of meeting people she knew in the waiting room. Having John accompany her seemed to add to the stress because he enjoyed running into everyone. It was difficult for her to stay hidden with a spouse who actively engaged people in conversation. Having John come to therapy helped the process even before he joined her in the session.

Dorothy's complaint about my being late touches on an area where she and I differed at times. It is not true that I am deliberately late in order to desensitize people. Dorothy is a stickler for promptness, but I sometimes get behind when patients need extra time or when crises come up during the day.

Differences that arise between therapist and patient sometimes provide fertile ground for working through similar issues in real life. I was probably not going to change significantly in this area to please Dorothy, and she was probably not going to let go of her need to start on time to please me. Learning to live with people who are different is a tough lesson for everyone.

Dorothy and John

Asking Dorothy to wait in the other room while I bonded with John is a typical way for me to begin couples therapy when I don't know one of the spouses. It's important to establish a relationship of trust with both partners so that neither person thinks I am colluding with the other. It was four months into therapy before Dorothy asked John to come in. I needed some time to get to know him before we worked together.

When Dorothy came back to the session, I asked them to look in each other's eyes and tell me three things they liked about each other. That task was easy for Dorothy and John, although it's sometimes very difficult for a couple who have been in crisis for some time. But John and Dorothy answered quickly and seemed to care for each other.

During that first interview one of the clues that this couple ever disagreed or became irritated with each other came when Dorothy decided she didn't like John swiveling in his chair, and she put her foot against it to stop the movement. I noticed John did stop swiveling.

I'm pretty good at detecting nonverbal cues even when I do not know the message behind them. I may have an idea about what the message is, but it's up to the person to give me that information. I don't assume I know what's going on without checking it out.

I pushed Dorothy to tell me why she put her foot on John's chair because she usually got to the meaning quickly. I didn't want to let her off the hook when she told me that she didn't know why she did that. Bringing a pattern or mode of communication to awareness helps the change process by helping discern whether or not it makes sense to continue that behavior. Learning to verbalize her wants and feelings instead of trying to get what she wanted through manipulation and control was something Dorothy wanted and desired.

Together and Separate

Dorothy did state a request clearly toward the end of the session. She wanted to continue working on her own issues during individual sessions while continuing to come in with John during couples sessions. There is no set pattern for how I work with patients. Individual, group, couples and family sessions are a few of the approaches I take to working with patients in therapy.

At PCS we also specialize in intensive outpatient treatment. We have found intensives to be especially helpful in treating patients who are "stuck" in the process of recovery or are facing a current crisis that necessitates more intensive therapeutic involvement. This is a two- to five-week program customized to the needs of the individual patient.

Dorothy and John did not seem to need our intensive program at that time, and we settled on a schedule that made sense for them and their family. I loved how Dorothy said what she wanted, and I felt great about continuing to work with her individually while seeing them as a couple. Since John agreed to that format, it's the direction we chose. It's important that the goals of therapy be a joint venture between patient and therapist. I do not set goals for patients, although I can help guide them through their own process.

Dorothy symbolically chose a pattern for therapy that became important to her in her life—separate and together. It is a pattern that rings true for me and has been important in my own life. Another symbol that reminds me of how important it is to maintain our separateness as well as our togetherness in marriage is the tradition in some marriage ceremonies of lighting the unity candle.

At some point in a marriage ceremony, bride and groom each light a candle. Then they move to a larger candle that they both light from their individual candles. Then they blow out their separate candles, signifying the unity they are creating through marriage.

As a pastor, I have married many couples. I have the bride and groom light the center candle and then keep their own candles burning. It's important that both bride and groom keep their individual personalities alive and growing even while they grow as a couple. It's not unusual for couples to come in because their individual flames have long been extinguished.

Telling Others
It took Dorothy four months to tell family members that she was in

therapy. We utilized role-playing activities to help her work through her fear of self-disclosure. Besides writing this book to share her experience with readers who might wonder about the therapy process, Dorothy obtained a master of counseling degree. It is always interesting to me to see where people go once they open themselves to new possibilities.

Therapy does not always mean a change in career, lifestyle or family. At best you'll end up where you want to be, which might be close to where you started. The maxim "Know thyself" expresses the general goal of therapy. How that works out for each patient is both an adventure and hard work. I never know where anyone will finally end up, and sometimes it comes as quite a surprise.

5

Anger
—Dorothy—

Dear God,

You gave me emotions to add to the richness of life's experiences. To express what I'm feeling and to alert me to something that's going on with me. Jesus said, "Out of the overflow of his heart his mouth speaks" (Luke 6:45). That speaks to me of emotion and its force in life.

Some people's emotions are encouraged and validated when they are children, and their lives are enriched by the full expression of those feelings. They are able to have a good overflow of the heart. With freedom they give words to the feelings within. And as they share those feelings, the overflow continues in other people.

For me the flow of emotion was damaged or destroyed by people whose emotional growth was damaged. There was no safety in showing my feelings. My emotions brought me only pain, and soon there was no overflow of the heart.

To compensate for the loss of that flow of emotion and to have enough strength to keep my emotions from overflowing, I learned different ways to speak. Out of those ways came behaviors that had nothing to do with feelings and had everything to do with performance.

That performance was sometimes destructive and sometimes constructive but always costly. Every now and then my emotions flailed against my heart, seeking an outlet. I had to try even harder to subdue them. I lost sight of the original goodness for which you created emotions.

The real tragedy is that my experience of feeling joy and love was lost because of my unwillingness to know sadness and sorrow. There was no balance between them for me. There was only the continuously painful overflow of my heart.

Just as people helped to cripple me, people must also help to heal me. When fears assail me, I resort to whatever safe emotions have been allowed to overflow my heart—fear or anger.

God, you know what can penetrate the callousness of my fortress heart. The ease with which others live out of the overflow of your gift of emotions is wonderful. I think they do not know what a gift it is. It's as natural to them as breathing.

I know that emotional support from others can help heal me. As they give of themselves to another, you increase what they have to give.

This is such a battle. Help me to accept the healing process of my life.

I love you,
Dorothy

"Dorothy, what's going on with you right now?" Ralph turned from his conversation with John to question me. I felt the welling of an intense rage that threatened to choke me. I looked at John and then at Ralph. Then I exploded with anger.

"I'm not listening to any of this from either of you anymore. You both keep saying the same thing over and over, and I'm sick of listening to you. You aren't listening to me, and you haven't heard what I've said." Ralph sat and listened to my tirade. I wanted to throw something at him. Something that was important to him. Maybe his stupid glass sculpture that sat in a corner. I was hurt, and when I'm hurt I rage.

"What is it I'm not hearing you say? Please tell me again."

"We keep going over the same old issue, and you keep giving the same advice that doesn't work, and you keep putting me in a position where I'm not protected." I was yelling and losing control.

Ralph tried again. "As I was talking to John, I noticed you looking around the room. I stopped to check on you to see what you were feeling. Can you tell me more?" I folded my arms and glared at Ralph. He had received "the glare" on many occasions, and it didn't bother him.

"Here comes the glare," he joked in an attempt to lighten the dark mood. Joking sometimes dissipated my anger, but not this time. I continued to glare at him until he said, "Dorothy, I need you to speak to me. I can't read your mind, and I have other patients waiting." He'd never said that before. He'd never hurried me in order to make time for other patients. I felt discounted and unimportant.

"Fine, go get your other patients," I said as I grabbed my stuff and headed for the door. I had been angry before, but I had never left mad. I think he knew that I did not intend to return.

"Dorothy, please wait a minute." My hand was on the doorknob. He didn't get up to follow me, but he was persistent about not ending the session this way. "I'm feeling some anxiety now, and I need you to stay. Will you please come sit down for a moment?"

I turned the doorknob. Why didn't he let me leave? Why didn't I just go? I felt panic and fear. The anger was dissipating, and I was afraid. "Dorothy, will you look at me for a moment?" he asked. I looked. "If you won't come back in, will you at least promise to schedule another appointment for next week?"

How could he read my mind? How did he know I had no intention of ever coming in again? "Yes," I barely whispered.

"What did you say? I couldn't hear you."

"Yes," I said again. And then I walked out. I thought a lot about the angry times in therapy. There were plenty of them to think about. I needed to feel safe before I expressed emotions. I didn't trust my feelings to be valid, nor did I believe I had a right to feel them. When I reflected on my outbursts, my emotions seemed childish.

I had developed my intellectual side and felt comfortable with it. When others wanted to communicate with me on an emotional level, though, I became uncomfortable and started to intellectualize or debate with them. Feelings seemed chaotic to me. When I did sense my emotions starting to surface, I generally switched to anger as a defense. People usually backed down when I presented an angry front. This pattern dominated even my most precious relationships. Parents who are out of touch with their own emotions can't model emotions for their children.

The important relationships in my own life were shaped by anger. Later I sought out the same kinds of people and perpetuated the anger. I had some destructive relationships that were based on the other person's anger. I thought that was how people related. It seemed normal to me, even though I was troubled by it.

I wanted to get rid of the anger and to experience other emotions without fear. Experiencing my anger with Ralph was healing. He helped me get past the anger and identify the emotion it covered. He never responded to my anger with his own. Sometimes he was frustrated with me, but he was never angry.

"Let's look at the picture collage you brought in." Ralph came over and sat beside me as we looked at a picture poster I had made as a homework assignment. We were talking about my previous marriage, which had been difficult and abusive. Ralph asked me to draw out the abusive aspects of it, but I found it easier to tape together pictures of the people and situations that triggered memories for me from that time.

But there was something different going on during this session. I felt uncomfortable with Ralph. Was he bored with the session? I asked him several times if he was mad at me or frustrated. "This is the third time you've asked me that. No, I'm not angry or frustrated," he said. His denial did nothing to help me feel more comfortable. Maybe it wasn't me. Maybe something else was going on. But it felt like me.

"Bob and Karen [fictitious names]," he said as he pointed to one of my pictures. I couldn't react. I froze. He knew someone from my past, and I didn't know what to do with that information. "How do you know them?" I asked.

He started telling me how he knew them. The more he talked, the more I panicked. I didn't trust the couple he recognized, and I could tell he liked them. Now he wouldn't believe me when I talked about them. When I tried to tell someone what was going on in the past, no one believed me. I tried to act normal, but I wouldn't give him more information. He knew I was upset.

"Tell me about this picture. What happened during that time?" He tried to move on. The only answers I could give were very brief statements or yes-and-no answers. My trust for Ralph, which I had valued above all, had fled. He was turning out to be just like everyone else after all.

Ralph tried to reconnect with me, even extending the session by fifteen minutes. I withdrew from him and threw up every wall I knew how to construct. There was no way he could penetrate the barriers. Finally, he stood up and said he needed to end the session. I gathered my stuff and headed for the door. He blocked my path and held his hand out to shake mine. I withdrew my hand for a moment, and he said, "Now I'm hurt." I quickly extended my hand because I didn't want him to know that I didn't know what I was feeling.

I walked to the front desk to pay for the session. When I got into my car, all I could think of was leaving everyone for a while. I was planning on flying to Chicago the next day to visit Celeste, but I decided to drive to Chicago that night instead. Driving was a great way for me to escape and think. Several times in the past I had loaded up the kids and driven to Florida or California when I needed to get away.

I called John to tell him that I was upset about something Ralph had said and that I was driving to Chicago. I wouldn't tell John what had upset me, but I wanted him to know I was safe and needed some time. I also asked John to call PCS and cancel all of my appointments, since I wasn't going back. He was great about giving me the time I needed to work through the tough issues when they came up. I could tell he was concerned about me.

I had driven as far as Flagstaff when a beautiful winter storm set in. I rented a room for the night and walked through the storm until I felt peaceful. I spent the rest of the evening writing and sorting through my feelings. When I called John, he said he had called Ralph because he was worried about me. Ralph asked that I call him as soon as possible so we could talk. He didn't tell John anything about the session.

"What happened to you?" Ralph asked when I returned to his office a week later.

"I felt threatened when you recognized that couple. I panicked and remembered how unsafe I was around them before. I thought if I had gone to you for help back then you wouldn't have listened to me or believed me."

"Dorothy, I would have listened and I would have believed you," he continued, telling me what I already knew. "I am very good at listening to a story and not taking sides. I would have believed you.

Anyway, I'm glad you rehired me." Emotions other than anger were starting to surface, and I had a safe place to experience them. Ralph was consistent in his regard for me, while I was all over the map with my feelings.

It never made sense to me to go to people and present them with a list of wrongs they did to me. I have done plenty to hurt others myself. The best I can hope for is to acknowledge what I've done and to forgive others for what they did to me. It's an ongoing process. Emotions can sometimes be experienced in therapy by dealing with whatever is going on in the here and now. I never had to confront those people about my feelings for them. It wouldn't have been productive, and I accomplished the same results by processing it with Ralph.

Later that month John waited for me in the reception area of PCS. We had a two-hour session scheduled for that day to work on an important issue. I had scheduled time several months ago to have a family session with a family member who was visiting during that time but had decided to use the session with John instead.

"Dorothy, the second hour of our session was given to another patient. The receptionist just told me so I could tell you," John said.

"What do you mean, given to someone else? I scheduled this months ago. We can't work through this in one hour. Tell her we don't want to switch," I insisted. John went to speak to the receptionist and returned to me. "She said it's Ralph's policy to give preference to a new patient over an old one. We can take the one hour or we can reschedule."

I couldn't believe Ralph would do this. He knew I had scheduled the two hours, and he didn't know I had decided not to bring someone else with me from out of town. I needed the two hours, and I didn't want to reschedule. I was barely getting by. I needed his help.

We walked outside and talked it over. Neither of us understood why Ralph would give away half of our appointment. After a few minutes Ralph came outside looking for us. "Dorothy and John, I'm sorry this happened. As my receptionist explained, your second hour was given to another patient. We can either use one hour of it or we can reschedule."

"Ralph, this isn't fair. You knew I had this time scheduled months ago. I need the two hours today." I felt desperate.

"Dorothy, this is a new patient who is coming in. I can't just cancel him and tell him to come back another time. I'm sorry this happened, but that's my policy. A new person usually takes precedence over an old one." He looked like he was becoming agitated with me. I didn't care. I couldn't believe what he was saying.

"Look, why don't we go to my office, and we can discuss this in there." We all filed into our usual seats. Our "token" hour was half over as it was. Ralph went to check on whether the new patient was going to show up. If he didn't, that would certainly solve part of our problem. When he returned he said, "The new patient is already here, so we can't use the second hour. We've already used up much of this hour too. Would you like to come back for one hour after this appointment? I can open that time for you."

"No, I don't want to come back for an hour later today. You probably have family things to do, and I need two hours, not one." My voice sounded shrill. This was not the Ralph I knew.

"This is a side of you I've never seen before," Ralph said to me. Unbelievable! He thinks I'm being unfair and rigid, and I'm thinking the same thing about him. Stalemate. We both just sat and stared at each other.

I gave it one more shot. "John, do you understand what I'm upset about?" I hoped John could communicate what I was trying to say. Ralph and I weren't getting anywhere with our conversation.

"Ralph, I think Dorothy and I heard you say that your policy is to give the second hour of a two-hour time slot to a new person who needs it."

"No," Ralph shouted and almost lunged out of his chair. "Is that what you thought I said?" He looked to me for confirmation.

"Yes, you said a new patient takes priority over an existing one."

"No, I would never take away your time. We had a computer glitch, and your time was given to this other person. If that happens, I have to make a decision about what to do. In that case, and only in that case, I think the new person takes priority. No wonder you were angry. I'd be furious." The old Ralph was back.

"And you thought I was being selfish and insensitive about a mistake. I understand this situation perfectly, and I'm glad to reschedule." This incident reminded us how tricky communication can be when emotions are involved, as they usually are. We all felt great about having toughed it out with each other until we understood what each person was trying to say. I felt good about the session we had, even though it wasn't the session we had planned.

—*Ralph's Notes*—

Dorothy's prayer about her emotions moved me deeply. It expressed the innermost depths of her soul. Her deepest feelings came through the safety of her prayers. She allowed herself to open up to me through her relationship with God. Therapeutic recovery became possible as she learned to be open and transparent about her damaged emotions.

Marilyn Murray is a therapist in our practice at Psychological Counseling Services. She is gifted at working with patients on healing their "inner child." Part of that process looks at the ways our "controlling child" develops in order to protect us from trauma and abuse in our early years. In Marilyn's theory of emotional development, our "controlling child" helped us create the defense mechanisms we needed to survive as children. But sometimes those same defense mechanisms interfere with adult intimacy.

Dorothy had a strong controlling child in place that kept her isolated and focused on achievement. She worked very hard to express herself through successes in work, school, church drama and numerous other activities. Her controlling child protected her well during her childhood and tried to protect her from the scary work of allowing intimacy into her life as an adult. Intimate relationships had almost always frightened Dorothy in the past. Persuading her controlling child to let go was a constant challenge in the beginning stages of therapy.

Part of the process of connecting to her "original feeling child" (Marilyn Murray's term for the child that freely feels emotions at birth) involved my being able to detect subtle body language shifts when Dorothy began to connect to her feelings. Dorothy looked upset when I asked her what was going on during our session with John.

There were several times when Dorothy complained to me and to John that we weren't hearing her. She would either explode and remove herself from the room or remove herself from our conversation by retreating into silence. When she thought about throwing something, she was expressing a healthy, honest reaction to feelings of being pushed to open up more. Her controlling child tried to prevent me from helping Dorothy get to deeper awareness of her emotions.

Sometimes Dorothy expressed fear of intimacy through rage. My desire as her therapist was to get her to articulate what was going on inside, what the rage was all about. I am usually pleased when a patient gets upset because the feelings expressed are authentic, if not pleasant. Dorothy's anger provided a demonstration of the way she sometimes operated outside the office as well as in relationships. Her moment of anger in therapy got her out of her head and into some real feelings, which are very important parts of recovery.

Passive Versus Aggressive

John became more quiet as Dorothy escalated, which demonstrated the way they interacted as a couple. Over the years, I have noticed that one spouse is usually passive-aggressive, while the other is more openly aggressive. The aggressive one becomes even more angry at the passivity of the other.

As Dorothy became louder and more angry, John became more quiet and looked at me as if to say, "Well, there she goes again." When Dorothy writes that it's almost as if he enjoyed letting her be the angry one, my belief about Dorothy and John is that at one level that was the case. His way with dealing with conflict differed from hers in not being explosive.

The Glare

Dorothy's glare didn't bother me. In fact, I have my own version of it. My glare has been used for "special occasions," not only on my personal family but also on my PCS family. I like to ask patients what their glare is about. Dorothy's glare produced a chilly atmosphere in the therapy session that was hard to miss.

Dorothy's glare and/or anger usually resulted in extended periods of silence. This particular time I tried to get past the silence more quickly than I would normally. I realize that I do react differently at times during therapy sessions. Sometimes the different reaction generates the energy needed to change a pattern. Other times it works less well.

During that particular session with Dorothy I believed I had joined sufficiently with her to be direct. I let her know that our time was limited and other patients were waiting. That form of directness has a certain amount of risk attached to it. I believe it is important for therapists to take risks at times. I try to do what is clinically sound and prayerfully carefront when necessary.

It was important to have Dorothy commit herself verbally to setting up another session so that she was not able to "nuke" herself by not returning. I wanted a commitment from her to come back the following week because I realized she was struggling with my response to her silence. I knew Dorothy would come back if she said she would, even if she didn't want to.

It's very important that therapists have the integrity of their own personality type and use therapeutic skills that fit each individual. That does not mean being a chameleon that changes to fit the personality of every client. It does mean being sensitive to the space and mood a patient is in while working to unlock potential and growth.

When Dorothy switched to anger as a defense, my style was to be fairly direct and carefront her anger to try to help her understand what her anger was about. Dorothy's anger didn't work in relation to other people at times, and it didn't work in therapy. I remember thanking her for allowing me to see her angry side, because my belief is that she would not have demonstrated her anger and rage if she had not felt comfortable enough to be that way with me. She certainly was well defended enough to present a calm exterior while keeping her emotions inside.

Collage Work

I find picture collages and other types of art therapy to be a tremendously helpful resource. When Dorothy asked me if I was mad or frustrated, I could honestly say that I wasn't. Therapists must be honest about what they are feeling when a patient asks. There were times when I admitted my frustration with her. It's not a fair contract to expect only the patient to be honest about what is going on.

When I recognized two people in her pictures, I mentioned that I knew them. Sometimes that makes sense to do and sometimes it doesn't. Occasionally I know someone a patient knows or talks about. It would not be therapeutic to mention former or current patients. The people I recognized on Dorothy's collage had never been patients of mine.

When Dorothy left upset because of the collage experience, I was reminded of training I did as a Ph.D. student. I was carefronted by my clinical pastoral education group. They told me I would have a major challenge as a therapist because I wanted to tie everything up at the end of the session into some kind of pretty package. It was uncomfortable for me to leave things unsettled, even if that would be more therapeutic. The feedback from my group has been helpful to me through the years as I have learned to "let go and let God" handle the orchestration of difficult sessions. I needed to learn not to overcontrol therapy sessions.

It was important that Dorothy continue to work on her anger and for me not to allow her to escape from those feelings until there was more understanding and change. Fast, temporary resolutions would not lead to the actual change necessary to prevent similar behavioral patterns in the future.

You're Fired/Rehired

It was meaningful to me as a therapist when Dorothy fired me and then decided to come back. It became clear to Dorothy that I wasn't that easy to get rid of and that she could go through her emotions, get angry, cancel appointments and then have the courage to come back.

It is super that she informed her husband John of the situation. It was considerate of him to let me know she was safe. Dorothy needed to get away from the situation and had a perfect right to take time to think and pray about her feelings. She took the time she needed to sort through her thoughts and emotions and then came back ready to continue her therapy sessions.

Nobody can know for sure what part of the therapy process is more growth producing—work done outside of session or the work that is triggered in session. The total picture was important for Dorothy in terms of her learning how to respond in ways that differed from her chronic pattern of anger and hurt.

When Dorothy canceled all the appointments she had made at

PCS, I realized how tremendously frustrated she was. I believed she would be back because we had a track record of working through issues over a period of a year and a half. I trusted Dorothy's commitment to continue doing what she needed to do to get to a better place. At times I trusted her more than she trusted herself, which is frequently the role I play as a therapist. I do know how much that dynamic meant to me when I was on the other side of the couch—times when my therapist believed in me even as I was having a difficult time believing and trusting myself.

Dorothy knew that she could fire me at any time but that I was not going to abandon her. Therapy was a safe place for her to "fire" someone who hurt her. In other relationships the effect could be longer lasting.

Walking Out
Sometimes it is difficult to know what to do when patients walk out of a session. I try to make the best decision clinically and prayerfully. At times it makes sense to keep them in the room until they get to a better place. Other times it makes sense to let them leave and then, perhaps, call to see how they are doing in between sessions. At other times it is productive to have a patient leave and then let the patient make choices about whether or not to reestablish contact.

There are a lot of judgment calls made on a regular basis when doing therapy in order to try to figure out what makes the most sense in a particular situation. Often I will talk to another therapist to check out my own impressions about what is best.

Communications Meltdown
The computer glitch, which caused another angry time between Dorothy and me, presented an opportunity for us to work through a communication mix-up. Those moments are very important to the

therapy process and present "real-time" issues that mirror life.

Dorothy wanted to look at intimacy issues with extended family members to see if relationships could become deeper and more meaningful. At the same time she and John were experiencing some critical issues in their own lives, and she needed extended time for a couples session. I let her decide how to spend the two-hour session. She had a lot of anxiety going into the session regardless of who she brought with her.

Dorothy has increased my awareness of the intense emotions that patients have before I meet with them. A new patient usually experiences anxiety about the intake session. But I didn't know about Dorothy's escalating anxiety regarding the session mix-up until I came out to the waiting room to get her. By that time she had gone outside to talk with John about their options. When I came to get them, she voiced her frustration about being bumped.

I tried to explain the situation to her, but we were both hearing different things from each other. I could not understand her refusal to be flexible, since my experience of Dorothy is that she can be extremely flexible when asked. There wasn't a lot of time left, and I was frustrated that we were stuck on the schedule conflict and were not in session.

I am thankful that John and Dorothy continued discussing their frustration so that we could get to the bottom of things. I am thankful to myself that I didn't nuke the whole session by cutting them off. There have been times when I was abrupt with patients and then made amends with them. Dorothy's comment that she felt good about the session we had even though it wasn't the session we planned is a great statement of how therapy works sometimes.

Since the beginning of my professional life as a therapist I have perceived myself as a relationship-centered therapist. Being person centered creates a risk of communication breakdowns. When there is a lot of emotional intensity behind any communication, it can be difficult to stay with the process in a way that is not hurtful.

Dorothy and I were able to unstick our communication through an awareness that we were experiencing each other in a way that wasn't consistent with our usual behavior toward each other. We were both confused about the inconsistencies we noticed in our messages. It was important to check out the meaning behind the words. John actually helped with that process as he reframed what Dorothy was trying to tell me.

It was excellent that John felt empowered to help his therapist understand what his wife was saying and that Dorothy agreed with her husband. Certainly in couples therapy it's an OK deal when the couple agree and work to help their therapist do a better job with them. John's message helped me hear what Dorothy was saying. When she felt understood, she was able to hear what I was saying. The session ended with our agreement to schedule another time and my offer to waive my usual fees for the session we had that day.

6

Things That Worked & Things That Didn't

—Dorothy—

Dorothy and John, I'd like you to consider taking a couples communication course together and an all-day couples group session. I think you are at a place where both would be very helpful," Ralph began.

"I don't do groups," I replied, "unless I'm the leader or it's a nonsharing type of group."

"I understand what you're saying, Dorothy, but I think you and John would find this experience helpful."

"What is an all-day group session like?" I asked.

"It's held here at my office on a Friday from 8:00 a.m. to 5:00 p.m. I'll be here with a group of couples, and I'd like you and John to be part of the group," he answered.

"Who's going to be in the group?"

"I can't tell you who the couples are. That's confidential, and you don't get a list beforehand."

"What if I know someone?" My anxiety about seeing people I

knew continued to run rampant.

"Then you'll know someone in the group."

Time to shift gears. I knew I wasn't going to get more information about the "guest list," so I pursued my interrogation. "What do you do for eight hours with a group of strangers?"

"It's similar to a regular group therapy session, but group members have to get to issues fast because of the time constraints. The couples usually report feeling connected by the end of the session. Even on the rare occasions when some participants knew each other, they still felt the group session helped," he explained.

"I think it would be an OK thing to try," John spoke up.

"Well, I don't. Maybe we could do the couples communication course but not the group session," I responded. "Tell me about the communication training."

"Couples communication is a four-week program designed to give couples skills to improve their communication with each other. Four to six couples meet on Thursday evenings from 4:00 p.m. to 8:00 p.m. We emphasize skill training, not working through issues. One of the therapists and his wife lead the sessions."

I liked the skill-training part. I could handle being with strangers as long as the conversation was superficial. "Let's do the couples communication course first, and if you are still convinced we need to attend the all-day session, then I'll think about it," I decided.

Ralph's arsenal of therapy techniques forced me into experiences that were outside my normal comfort zone. As awkward as I felt at times, the variety of techniques pushed me past troubling feelings or behaviors.

We arrived at our first couples communication session and sat with four other couples in the waiting room. We checked in and were given a book and the materials for the session. I liked this already. Anything with a book connected to it seemed like fun to me. I loved school, learning and reading.

While we waited, John began to make the rounds in the room, introducing himself and exchanging pleasantries. I became caught up in the lighthearted atmosphere of the conversation and joined in. This was different from the experience of waiting for therapy.

At 4:00 p.m. a tall, attractive young man came into the waiting area and introduced himself with a smile. "Hi, I'm Marcus Earle, and I'm facilitating your couples communication sessions with my wife, Robin. We're ready for you if you'd like to come back." Then he moved toward Ralph's office. That was the first time I had seen Marcus since the father-son talk he had presented with his father at Grace Community Church.

Inside, a charming, petite woman greeted us as she finished arranging the extra seats needed to accommodate our group. "Hi, my name is Robin Earle. I'll be coteaching with Marcus during the next four weeks. Please fill out a name tag and find a comfortable seat. We'll begin in a moment."

A delightful and warm person, Robin had an engaging smile that put me at ease. I felt "safe." Marcus was more reserved but was approachable. He had a sense of humor that often caught me off guard.

Robin taught us new techniques as we reviewed our homework assignments. We learned talking skills such as speaking for self, expressing thoughts, sharing feelings and disclosing wants. Active listening skills included summarizing, inviting the speaker to give more information and attending to the message with openness. Throughout the week we were to read, study and role-play the skills we had learned. During the session Robin and Marcus demonstrated the skill that we were to practice.

"OK, if there aren't any questions after our break, we'll be in small groups to practice the communication tools we've just learned," Robin directed. Coffee, cookies, brownies and friendly conversation made the sessions fun even as we learned new skills.

Even though the communication techniques were great tools in therapy, I often forgot to use them if John and I were well on our way to a fight. At that point neither of us wanted to be effective communicators; both just wanted to win. I once asked Marcus and Robin how they handled that problem in their life together.

"You're right, Dorothy. These techniques work if and when we choose to use them. Robin and I sometimes get caught up in being angry and decide not to use the skills. I find that talking about issues, using the techniques we've learned, becomes easier if you practice on a regular basis using everyday events. When a heated topic does come up, we may be more inclined to stay in a positive communication cycle," Marcus explained.

Couples communication worked for me in therapy, but couples group session didn't work. After we finished the communication training, Ralph brought up the all-day couples session again. "The couples session has room for one more couple. Have you made a decision about attending?" How I had been dreading that question!

John and I seemed to be uncovering things we didn't like about each other faster than a monkey can peel a banana. Our sessions with Ralph were becoming repetitive and irritating, at least to me. Ralph tried hard to help us move past our frustrations, but he ended up being part of the cycle. "Yes, I'll do the all-day thing. I don't want to come to therapy with John right now because it doesn't seem to be helping. But I'll give this a try." I was resigned to my fate.

Will Rogers once observed that it really doesn't matter who you marry, since it always turns out to be somebody else the next morning anyway. For John and me, the next morning dawned ten years later. For the first ten years of our marriage, we were too integrated into each other's space and activity to realize we didn't know each other. We worked together, played together, took care of the house and kids together, vacationed together, ate, slept, thought, talked and "breathed" together. Yet neither one of us felt accepted and loved by the other. Too busy to notice.

A pattern established itself in our sessions with Ralph. "I can't believe you said that," John yelled.

"Said what? What did I say?" I yelled back.

"You told me to get up and get you a glass of water, and if I didn't, you'd be furious," he declared.

"I did not! I asked you to get me a drink of water, and I did not threaten you in any way. You always hear things I don't say."

From here it often got ugly, with one of us accusing the other of acting just like his or her mother, brother, father, sister or whoever it was that the other most detested being likened to. Ralph refereed a game nobody would ever win. We needed to try something else, hence the group.

Friday morning found John and me at PCS for our all-day session. I had already met the other group members during two different pregroup sessions. Those sessions acquainted us with the group experience and introduced us to each other. The presessions were experiential and casual. Nevertheless, I was anxious. We had worked on some art therapy projects designed to help us know ourselves more and to share that awareness with the group. For one of the projects we drew or pasted pictures from magazines that symbolized the following areas of our lives: work, play, sexuality and spirituality. It was helpful to share with the other group members through the medium of art.

As we waited in the reception area, there wasn't much conversation. Knowing Ralph would be part of the group reassured me, since he knew my fears about sharing with others and would help me enter the process in a safe way. If I was silent, he would know how to help me say what I wanted to say. Then Ralph came to greet us and we all filed into his office. There was a scramble for the comfortable seats. John and I sat in the two swivel chairs, and the group arranged itself in a circle.

Ralph led off with a question: "How were the two previous nights of group for you?" Some shared their group experiences, offering feedback about what they liked, what they didn't like, and what insights they gained. I said nothing. I felt tense and was trying to anticipate what would happen next. John, on the other hand, laughed, shared and connected with the group.

"Let me talk about what we are going to do today," Ralph interjected after fifteen minutes of our settling in. "First, I'd like each of you, as couples, to say one or two things you like about the other. I know some of you are in a difficult place where that will be hard to do, but if you can reach deep inside to find something positive, please do." Ralph paused and asked, "Which couple would like to go first?"

"We'll go first," John blurted out.

OK, I thought, *this is something we can do without fighting.*

John easily identified two or three things he liked about me, and I did the same for him. As we waited for the next couple, I was thinking this "group stuff" was going to be a breeze.

"If they like each other that much, what are they doing here?" came a query from the group. Similar questions followed. "I guess they were the wrong couple to begin this exercise," Ralph chuckled. "Actually, I have them here as shills or decoys for the group," he kidded.

The morning flew by, and I was OK with the group experience so far. John and I enjoyed a relaxed lunch together and exchanged our perceptions about the session. John had shared and talked, but we really didn't understand what we were supposed to accomplish. I still had not shared in any way.

Since I didn't know the rules, I didn't know what was acceptable. Were we allowed to express disagreement? Anger? Doubt? Since I didn't know what it was OK to say, I didn't say anything.

The afternoon session was intense for most of the participants. I began to feel agitated and angry. These people were beginning to bother me with their incessant sharing. I wasn't saying anything, and no one expressed any concern about my silence. Most of all, I was angry with Ralph. He had convinced me to participate against my will, and now he ignored me.

With twenty-five minutes left in the session, Ralph turned to me and said, "Dorothy, what's going on with you?" He posed the question casually, as if there were actually time to explore my feelings. I became panicky and angry at the same time. Everyone stared at me silently, waiting for me to open up. I didn't feel connected to anyone in the room, and I wasn't going to share anything with them.

I glared at Ralph and said, "I'm fine. Nothing's going on with me." Suddenly everyone's attention was focused on me.

"Look at her glaring at Ralph." "Why are you here if you aren't going to participate?" "You can't communicate without anger, and I'm worried about how you are with your kids." "I shared deeply today, and you just sat there swiveling in that chair." The explosion of comments disoriented me. I wanted to leave, but I waited for the few minutes remaining in the session.

"Dorothy's feeling hurt and angry, and I know when she leaves here she is going to take that with her." John tried to explain my feelings to the group. "The rest of you have been able to share and will leave feeling pretty good, but it's difficult for her to share."

At least John had tried to defend me. Ralph, who knew better than anyone what my silence was about, only said, "Does anyone have anything else to share before we close? If not, remember our sharing is to remain in this room. Thanks for being in the group." Then he got up and left the room.

I grabbed my purse and ran out. I felt cheated and abandoned, and I wanted to put distance between myself and everyone else. On the way home I told John to go to a party that evening without me. I was so angry at Ralph that the party was ruined for me. And I was angry at him for that too.

I called my friend Connie and asked her to go to the mountains with me for the weekend. She was the person I shared my therapy experiences with, and she knew when I needed to debrief after difficult sessions. I could talk or not talk with her, and I could work through my anger without appearing childish or confused.

John was good about giving me the time I needed to sort through things and figure out where my turmoil was coming from. The group session left me feeling fragile and exposed. I felt as if I had just flunked something I had no idea how to pass. While I dealt with my feelings, I wrote some reflections I titled "Random Thoughts to God."

Why do you love me? Almost everyone who knows me intimately doesn't. If you would explain why you love me, then maybe I could tell them why they are wrong to reject me.

Winter is my favorite season. I feel close to you and I feel safe.

My children keep me from running away. Sometimes I resent that.

Relationships are complicated and painful. Where did the fun go?

I love writing. It is the most free thing I do. No one can twist what I say when it is in print.

People love men who are sensitive and emotional. They do not like women who are logical and intellectual.

Cycles exist and cycles are powerful: ocean tides, seasons, years, life and death. Can we really alter the cycles we get established in as children?

Sex is fun and doesn't cost anything, yet it costs everything.

Joy is eternal and transcends experience, and it's nice to share with another person.

Just as I scale one peak, I sight another one to climb. Scaling peaks is tiring, and not very many people want to toil along with you.

I like roses, candles, lunching with friends, laughing with Celeste, talking to Dan, playing with Julie, walking on the beach with John, reading, writing, praying, having my hair combed. Being understood!

I don't like fighting, crying, cleaning. Leaving therapy depressed!

If I had it all to do over again, would I change anything? You bet—in a heartbeat. I think people lie when they say they wouldn't.

Lord, do you understand my sadness? Ralph wants my marriage to work. Does he want me to work?

It's almost my birthday. Thanks for creating me, loving me, never giving up on me, hearing me.

In two weeks I returned to see Ralph. "Ralph, why didn't you help me talk during group?" I began. "You know I have problems sharing. I felt totally unprotected and was unprepared for the reactions I got from the other people."

We talked about the experience and the roles we each played in it. "I grade myself a C-minus in retrospect," Ralph said. "I think I did not do a great job in helping you, even though you were very clear about your fears."

Someone important in my life had seemed to let me down, but I survived. I learned something about how people perceived my silence. Ralph said they might have thought that I was rejecting them. I often think that aloofness may be an expression of shyness or fear, not haughtiness.

Six months later Ralph suggested another group. "I was wondering if you two could come to California next week. I am cofacilitating a week of intimacy work at Rancho Capistrano, which is a beautiful setting. It would give you time away together as well as time to explore some of your issues in a relaxed, tranquil atmosphere. Why don't you talk it over and let me know by tomorrow?"

It was indeed short notice, but sometimes that is the best way to take advantage of opportunities that present themselves. Yet hearing the words *couples* and *group* in the same sentence made my spine tingle with apprehension.

John and I decided to take a week of vacation and go for it. There would be lots of time during the stay to relax and enjoy ourselves, and if there's one thing John and I knew how to do well it was play. We arrived at the ranch early in the day and had several hours by ourselves before the seminar began that evening. The grounds were exquisite, and we walked until we were relaxed. I wasn't ready to meet the other couples, so I went back to our room to get ready.

The first evening we met together for a few hours to become acquainted. We each brought a symbol from home that described who we were. I brought a picture of the ocean with waves crashing against rocks on the shore. When it was my turn to share, I said, "This picture is of the ocean, which is the most peaceful place for me to be. I think I am like the ocean because I am consistent in many ways, like the tides. I present a peaceful image to others, like the smooth surface of the ocean in the background. Sometimes I have an undercurrent of feelings that are powerful and crashing, like the waves against the rocks."

John brought a video of *Peter Pan,* which he said symbolized his difficulty facing responsibility and growing up. He definitely likes to play.

For the next week we spent mornings together with Ralph and Marilyn (Ralph's coleader) as they shared skills and techniques with us concerning intimacy and relationships. During the afternoon we worked in small groups to practice the skills. The rest was free time.

The evenings were fun. We worked on a murder mystery and learned to square-dance. One night we went into town in search of "toys" or something to delight the inner child in us. John and I found out our inner children had expensive tastes, so we brought along our "inner adults" to help monitor what we spent.

On the last day we shared our experiences and the drawings we had made during the week. Emotional breakthroughs occurred as barriers came down amid tears and laughter. But I felt some discomfort. Even though I had spent a week getting to know the people in this group, I resisted being transparent with them.

The picture I drew showed me as a child in a place I considered safe—my closet—where I was reading a book. When I drew the picture, I felt unsafe, so I put locks on the closet. One lock didn't make me feel safe enough, so I put on several of them. Then I added chains with padlocks on them. Just for good measure, I added two armed guards. Finally, I began to cover up the little girl with crayon until the only thing left of her was her head. Then I felt comfortable and safe.

Finally I realized why I "stay in my head" when I share. Emotions made me vulnerable, and I was still afraid to release them. I shared the picture and the story with the group, and I cried. I couldn't believe the positive feedback I received from everyone. They said I seemed more real and less perfect. I passed group.

—Ralph's Notes—

What do you do in an all-day group session? That kind of question is asked frequently, and I expected it from Dorothy. She wanted as much information as possible before agreeing to embark on anything new in the therapy process. She found therapy itself mysterious and scary. It was something she had not counted on doing in her life. Whenever I presented her with a new situation or activity, she resisted it until she achieved some degree of comfort with it.

Sometimes I do not give couples enough information when I suggest that they do an intensive, or all-day, group session. Over the years I have become so familiar with the process that I tend to neglect explaining it initially. I need to give patients the data that they need to make the best decisions for themselves.

Who's going to be in the group? When a patient asks this question, I cannot answer. It is unethical for a patient list to be seen by anyone other than the therapists involved and the office staff. It came as no surprise when Dorothy asked that question. She had been apprehensive about running into people she knew ever since therapy began. It is normal and understandable for patients to ask who will be in a group setting with them. In a city the size of Phoenix it is still possible to run into someone you know. Dorothy often ran into people she knew in the waiting room.

I may not put someone in a group if that person has a close friend who is already in it. I won't put a pastor in a group if a member of the congregation is in it. But it's not always easy to keep acquaintances out of the same group. It has been known to happen that two couples who know each other fairly well discover that they are scheduled to be in the same group. In those cases I have left it up to the couples to decide whether or not they care to continue the process. Most of the couples in this situation have decided to go through the process together. Many times it helps them get over their fear of allowing others to know them intimately.

Couples Communication Program

Dorothy and John had their choice of resources to help them work on their issues. Their communication needed to improve, and we have a wonderful course designed to help couples in that area. The Couples Communication Program (CCP) is designed by Sherod and Phyllis Miller and is used extensively in our therapy approach. The course continues to be updated by the Millers and has proven to be extremely helpful in terms of outcomes—improvement in couples communication skills.

Many couples think they must be great communicators because they communicate at work. John and Dorothy presented well in front of large audiences and with clients in their profession. But everyone who has ever taken the communication course (and has done the homework) has benefited from the techniques and skills presented in it.

One of the advantages of CCP is that it is educational therapy and provides specific skills that participants can learn and transfer to daily interactions. John and Dorothy are both very intelligent, and this course provided them an opportunity to learn new skills. The course is particularly beneficial for couples who actively seek solutions and for those who enjoy continuing education.

Marcus's humor frequently catches people off guard, including me. Marcus sometimes uses paradoxical intention when he does therapy. Clients are generally encouraged to change by direct and straightforward procedures. There are times, however, when clients resist making changes. The use of paradoxical intention invites change through the use of contradictory statements or responses. As Marcus's father, I feel privileged to function as a cotherapist with him in four different ongoing groups.

Couples Intensive

At the time when John and Dorothy were in therapy, we worked with couples in all-day intensive types of therapy. Five or six couples worked with two or three therapists for an entire day or longer. Part of the process at that time included a presession with a therapist who specialized in art therapy. The couples were introduced to each other and the group process in an attempt to alleviate some of the anxiety regarding the group experience.

John and Dorothy were stuck in patterns that had become deeply ingrained over the ten years that they had been together. I understood the frustration in Dorothy's comment that we didn't seem to be getting anywhere. I have experienced that as a patient in my own therapy and as a therapist with other clients. Couples work includes three entities —in this case, Dorothy, John and the relationship. I do my best to avoid colluding with either partner. I try to work in the best interest of both parties with the goal of creating a healthy relationship.

One of the interesting aspects of couple relationships is the different personalities involved. Part of what attracted Dorothy and John to each other was their complementary differences. John is a salesman and knows how to connect with people. He is quick to engage with others and can easily talk to strangers as well as acquaintances. It was easy for him to adapt to a new situation such as group therapy, in which he was called upon to connect with others. Part of him liked to share intimately and part of him liked to perform before the audience.

Dorothy took the whole process so seriously that she read into everything more than was there, reflecting on questions like *What does he think about me? Why am I here? What did she mean by that comment?* and so on. Taking every comment to such a deep level created anxiety early in the process.

John and Dorothy had a lot in common when it came to leadership skills and presenting before an audience. Demonstrating what was really going on inside was frightening to both of them in different ways. Dorothy didn't want to disclose anything, and John wanted approval for the many ways he did disclose.

Group Humor
When I said that I had engaged John and Dorothy as shills, I was trying to inject some humor into the group experience. If I modeled the use of laughter into the process, the group members might be freed up to do so when necessary and appropriate. The all-day process can be draining emotionally, and a good laugh can lighten the atmosphere. It is never helpful to use laughter to deflect deep feelings. Sharing laughter, as well as tears, is helpful to the process.

Group Share
People share in differing degrees and styles in group therapy. The group often mirrors how people operate in life because of the intensity of the experience. In the beginning participants check each other out and try to act appropriately. Somewhere along the process people settle into their own mode of operation. It is difficult to keep up a pretense in a group situation.

I was aware of Dorothy's silence in the group situation, just as I am aware of it in our individual sessions. Her silence can mean lots of things, so I usually check on that. In this case I let the group handle her silence with their own responses. Her silence was very loud to the group. I decided against bailing her out because I trusted her inner strength to deal effectively with the group. I didn't want to make the path too easy for her, yet I didn't want her to be overwhelmed either. I have great trust in the group process, and I believed that John and the others in the group would help Dorothy and me create a safe environment to do something she had never done before—trust a group of people with her innermost thoughts and feelings.

It was good to have a cotherapist compliment Dorothy for staying with the process instead of leaving. That therapist shared an experience of being tempted to bail out of a group session she once participated in as a patient. Dorothy received validation for her part in the group, which was being able to stay in the group despite her fear.

It was interesting to hear John say some things in Dorothy's defense. I perceived his actions to be loving and caring, not codependent. His message to the group and Dorothy was a message of empathy for her and an awareness of how she felt.

I love Dorothy's "Random Thoughts to God," in which she expresses her feelings about the group experience. Again she used her writing to release her sense of having been abandoned by me during the group process and her need to figure out what happened. Dorothy often made significant changes when she confronted her fears. Once she identified a pattern or mechanism that wasn't working in her life, she worked hard to change it.

In her piece Dorothy comments that "Ralph wants my marriage to work" but wonders, "Does he want me to work?" There is a fine line to walk when working with couples and their relationships. I am biased because I like to see relationships improve. I always tell patients that, since I want to be up front about my biases. If Dorothy and John did not want their relationship to improve, then the question would be, Why are we doing couples therapy? In their case they did want things to improve. It is helpful for the therapist and the patient to have the same goals.

My challenge to John and Dorothy was to use the ingredients they had to improve the recipe in their marriage. I made it clear to them that I would continue to be available to do individual therapy with one or both if they did decide to end the marriage. Dorothy asked me that question at a time when the outlook for their marriage was clouded. The fact that both are committed to the process of working toward a better place greatly improves the chances that their marriage will stay healthy.

GRADE: C-minus

I believe that in a relationship style of therapy nothing is gained by trying to present myself as a person who always does the right thing in therapy. Dorothy came back after the couples group telling me she felt unprotected and unprepared for the process. I listened to her and told her that I gave my own participation in the group a grade of C-minus.

Many judgment calls are made during the therapy process, and I don't think I did a good job of preparing Dorothy for her experience. I probably missed an opportunity to help her early in the group process when I did not invite her to share with the group. Instead I waited until the end of the day, when her anxiety and fear had increased to very high levels.

I often have to take a mental break during therapy to think, stop, listen and pray for God's guidance because of the importance of being the best coach I can for each individual. I know how angry I get at referees who appear to make a wrong call during a game on TV. Yet I have tremendous empathy for that kind of job, because in many ways a therapist makes judgment calls that can be very difficult.

The Ranch

Timing is important to the therapy process. I can't pretend to know what would be the best time for patients to work on issues in their lives or in what setting. I can't always rely on the patient to know either. Sometimes it happens synchronistically and comes as a surprise to me and the patient. The experience at Rancho Capistrano appeared to be a great fit for John and Dorothy. When a slot opened up for them, they agreed to take it.

The opportunity to work with Marilyn Murray and John and Dorothy in a different setting was serendipitous for me. The change of venue and the beautiful setting created an experience that was fun, creative and safe for John and Dorothy to continue their work as a couple. The seminar was hosted by the Crystal Cathedral in Garden Grove, California.

Many of the sessions at the ranch provided Dorothy with opportunities to get more inside herself and understand more about "little Dorothy." As she got more in touch with her child within, she empowered herself as a feeling adult in the present. Dorothy has a playful side that was seldom engaged during her intense working times. She pursued her goals with such persistence that she forgot to enjoy the journey.

A major breakthrough in Dorothy's therapeutic process came when she understood her tendency to stay in her head by intellectualizing and debating. She made progress toward the ability to connect her gut with her head. She also learned that when she shared herself honestly and tears came from deep inside, others were able to connect with her from their own "sobbing, hurting child."

I loved the opportunity that presented itself throughout the week at Rancho Capistrano. I appreciate the spontaneity and flexibility John and Dorothy showed by agreeing on such short notice to take a week from their busy schedule to travel to California. They took a risk and something good happened.

7

Termination
Trauma
—*Dorothy*—

T*ime is running out, and panic overwhelms me. Early in the day John and my sister Barbi want to experience the hugeness of the city, and I am pulled along with them. We run into a deli and then a bookstore. We shop until I become so disoriented that I tremble with fear. In a museum we become separated and spend hours searching for each other among the statues and paintings.*

There is no time to get to her. I see her in the distance, waiting and beckoning to me to hurry. I run and leave everything behind in a frantic search through the maze of people and streets. My heart races because I know this will be my last chance. She remains visible but unreachable. Frantically I work my way through the mass of humanity bent on keeping us apart.

I reach the pier as dusk turns to darkness, only to see the last ferry depart. I stand paralyzed with fear and dismay. I can see her, but I can't reach her. That all-too-familiar sense of loss envelops me as I stare into the night.

I always wake up at this point in the dream. I have been in that same place with different people and events since I was sixteen years old. The outcome was always the same: I can't reach her—the Statue of Liberty. To me it was clear the dream was about the lack of freedom in my life. I had this dream whenever I felt stressed or trapped.

It had always been my goal to go to New York and spend time with that great symbol of freedom before I reached the age of forty. I accomplished my goal the same week I turned forty. When I returned, I looked forward to sharing that experience with Ralph in my next session.

"Ralph, my trip to Manhattan was perfect. We stayed at the Marriott Marquis on Times Square and saw and did as much as we could with every minute we had. It is the most incredible city. I love it." My enthusiasm was obvious as I told him about my "dream" trip. "It was a perfect time to visit the statue. Because it was so cold, there were no lines of people waiting to climb to the top," I continued. "I haven't had my New York dream for a long time, so this trip symbolized my growth and healing."

I enjoyed sharing my adventures and fun times with Ralph. My life wasn't entirely dominated by struggle and pain. I couldn't wait to tell him about my trip because I knew he enjoyed the excitement and energy of New York.

"Dorothy, I think it's time for you to consider terminating therapy. You have grown beautifully and have come to a good place to consider ending. Things seem to be going well for you. You have many skills and talents to draw on in working through the struggles and opportunities of your life. Of course, you can come back whenever you feel stuck," he added.

Suddenly I felt dizzy and disoriented. "Terminate"? What did being terminated have to do with New York? We had never mentioned Ralph's terminating me. I was under the impression that I would choose when I wanted to end therapy, which was probably never.

"Yes, terminate therapy. You're ready, I think," he added carefully.

We continued talking until our time was over. I don't know what I said or how I managed to focus on our conversation because I felt nauseated. How horrible the word *terminate* sounded! Terminate: abolish, cease, end, expire, finish. *Stop!* I felt like Alice in Wonderland when the king told her to begin at the beginning and go on till she came to the end—and then stop.

Outside I started the car and then just sat there, overwhelmed with grief. Waves of emotion washed over me as I struggled to regain my composure. I felt out of control. When I got home, I wrote the following prayer in my journal:

Dear God,

Here I am doing some of my favorite things: writing my thoughts and feelings to you, listening to Pachelbel and crying. I guess I'm being a bit sarcastic. I'm not sure what I'm writing about and even less sure what I'm feeling.

This is so ridiculous. What am I feeling? I guess I'm feeling rejected and lonely. Why? Ralph suggested I terminate therapy. That's a good thing, isn't it? It caught me off guard. Why?

It feels like having someone care about me and then leave. Having someone begin to know me and then leave. This is crazy. Knowing another person ends up feeling lonely.

This isn't even real. Losing my father-in-law was real. He loved me and I loved him, and now he's dead. You didn't need him, I did! Why do you always end relationships that bring me joy?

I don't want to be vulnerable ever again. *Ever.* I hate this. I hate this worse than anything. I'm not making sense even to me.

Here's what's logical. Ralph suggested we terminate therapy or at least begin the process of terminating because I'm doing so well. He's not rejecting me. We have a patient-psychologist relationship that helps me deal with other relationships. Ending therapy is a good thing.

I'm really tired. You expect too much of me. My life has been a series of rejections, and you're seeing how well I cope with it this time. How big does my wall have to get before you quit blasting it?

I know you care about me, but I don't feel cared for at the moment.

You know what's funny? I'd like to know what Ralph thinks I've succeeded at so far. I flunked group therapy, I write my feelings instead of talking about them, and I've barely begun to share who I am with others. To top it all off, I have this enormous reaction to his suggestion that I terminate therapy. Is that a sign of emotional health?

This letter is one of the most difficult I've written since being in therapy. I guess rejection is the real problem for me. I should have brought up terminating therapy before Ralph did. His bringing it up caught me off guard.

Therapy has provided a model for interacting that I never had. I see it as my checkpoint for good communication and relationship modeling. When you have had a dysfunctional childhood, you aren't even aware of distortions or behaviors that block intimacy. So in that sense, Ralph has helped me replace old ways of relating with good, nurturing ways.

I'm just not good at feelings, and I hate not being good at something. Period. Ralph said I should look at reasons why I think I still need therapy or present a case for continuation. I don't want to do that. It's asking for help, and I don't want to ask for help anymore. Besides, I could create all kinds of problems if I wanted to, but I don't want to.

I know I'm not making sense again. You tell me what you want me to do. I didn't want therapy in the first place. This reaction makes no sense.

I guess I don't have anything else to say. How am I supposed to get what I need? I think my strength and my ability to succeed sometimes get in the way of people's responding to my needs. They don't see any need in me. Not even Ralph!

I miss my father-in-law so much. He saw the needy part of me and loved me despite it.

Dorothy

P.S. I can't believe I'm writing a postscript to God. I recognize that Ralph is being conscientious in not having therapy continue too long. It is costly. I love you, and I'm grateful for all that you give me. I'm just sad at the moment, and I don't know why. I know one thing for sure—having you involved in my therapy keeps me honest.

In his book *Further Along the Road Less Traveled* M. Scott Peck observes that the termination of a relationship between a patient and a therapist can symbolize the whole issue of death and can give the patient an opportunity to work through death. I don't know if the thought of termination brought up my issues about death, but it did bring up issues of abandonment. I had never allowed myself to get close to people in order to avoid the risk of being abandoned. I kept my relationships on an intellectual level or I allowed someone to share intimately with me while keeping myself hidden and inaccessible. If a relationship broke, I didn't repair the damage. It was nothing for me to walk away from someone rather than admit to being hurt.

The only relationships I ever invested myself in emotionally were with my children and John. But I kept myself hidden even from them. I feared exposing my deepest fears and feelings. When Ralph gently suggested terminating our relationship, I was, for the first time, caught off guard. I didn't realize I had opened myself up to such overwhelming feelings. I felt an accumulation of all the fear and panic I had suppressed for forty years. In a way it was about death—the death of my protective walls and barriers to intimacy.

It was a turning point for me in therapy. I could block the emotions and walk away, or I could work through the pain with Ralph. This time the pain was about him.

"Ralph, I don't want you to terminate our therapy." I began facing my fears at our next session.

"Dorothy, have you identified areas in which your fear keeps you from doing something?" he asked.

"My fear about being terminated almost kept me from coming back to talk," I offered.

"OK, that gives us a place to focus our attention and work," he suggested.

"But I don't want you to be able to terminate therapy unless I'm ready. Even if I don't have anything profound to talk about. Even if I just want to sit and talk about nothing for an hour. Even if you are bored beyond belief with me. Even if I'm not remarkable, funny, intense or accomplished. Even if I sit and say nothing—forever!" I insisted.

With the beginning of a grin he answered in mock seriousness, "Dorothy, would you feel better if we reserved a standing appointment for you once a month until you are one hundred years old?" I folded my arms and dared him to say he wouldn't. We both laughed and therapy continued.

We worked through some of the solitary places of my life—places we had not touched before because keeping them hidden seemed safe. Out of the trauma of termination came an unanticipated healing.

For Jesus had commanded the evil spirit to come out of the man. Many times it had seized him, and though he was chained hand and foot and kept under guard, he had broken his chains and had been driven by the demon into solitary places. (Luke 8:29)

Dear God,

This Scripture describes what goes on in my mind when I'm not free from the demons of a distorted and destructive past. My past kept me wrapped in chains without my ever knowing it. But I knew that I hurt.

Many times the demons from my past seized me and overpowered my life. My response was to retreat to the solitary places of my mind, even in the presence of many people. They didn't notice my withdrawal, which heightened the solitariness of my retreat to a safe place.

It was a place of safety, but it was not a place of healing. It simply allowed me to get the demons back in chains. But it takes energy to keep the demons in check. So they are, in effect, actually controlling me instead of being controlled. And because I don't want to acknowledge their power over me, I can't even deal with them.

That's why Jesus brought them out into the open. He knew that identifying them and calling them by name would cancel their influence over me. Their power existed only as long as they were allowed to remain anonymous, only as long as I looked away from them. But denying the demons of my past is very dangerous. They even determine how I act or react to you.

They have no power in the light of your grace. When you decide it's time to name a demon or a force from my past, you also see me through the process.

I need the courage to not retreat into the solitary places. I must walk into the light instead. The light seems frightening because I'm not used to exposure. But I'm not alone in the light or the healing process. You send me precious guides who recognize the demons within me. They understand that the demons are not part of who you created me to be. They rejoice with me when they are banished.

Love,
Dorothy

—*Ralph's Notes*—

W hen patients bring in a dream, I sometimes ask them to interpret it. Or I may ask them to reenact parts of the dream. Some patients I may refer to a therapist who specializes in dream analysis.

Dorothy did not bring her dream to session. I knew of her desire to go to New York because it had come up in therapy. New York is one of my favorite cities, and we had talked about some of our shared interests there. When Dorothy returned from her trip, I enjoyed hearing about her adventures. As she talked, I noticed that she seemed to be at a good place in her life.

She seemed to be moving to a place where termination made sense for her. As I continued to listen to her, I decided to go with the termination theme as soon as she finished talking about her trip. Clearly, my mention of termination shocked her, although she tried to recover and act nonchalant.

After that I found it difficult to reconnect with Dorothy on any level. She withdrew in a powerful way and answered my questions with short, deliberate statements. I tried to pull her back into the session by discussing the process of termination, but she wouldn't enter into any meaningful communication with me. I knew I had struck a chord deep within Dorothy that she would probably need time and space to work through. I did my best to reassure her that she could continue to discuss any issues that were pressing her and suggested that she make a list of those needs.

The word *terminate* is probably not the best one to apply to the process of ending therapy. In our first session I had told Dorothy that I am an impatient person who tries to terminate therapy in the shortest time possible. And by this time Dorothy was, in fact, doing much better. My hunch was that she was moving to a place where the termination of therapy would be a positive step for her.

I was interested in celebrating the constructive changes Dorothy had made, and I was concerned that she not develop a dependence on therapy. One of her strengths was her ability to use her own resources as well as those available to her through family, friends and church.

Termination is usually a mutual decision based on the best interests of the patient. My intention certainly was not to cut Dorothy off without ever seeing her again. At that time I wanted her to begin to look at any remaining therapeutic issues and to focus on reasons for continuing therapy.

I asked Dorothy to think about her goals and consider why or why not it would make sense to end the process of formal therapy. Looking back, I realize that Dorothy got stuck on the word *terminate* and blocked out any further input from me. Knowing Dorothy well by that time, I was able to pick up on her anxiety even though she was doing her best to mask it. I was certainly not interested in exacerbating her sense of abandonment.

Abandonment

The letter Dorothy wrote to God about termination revealed her inner struggle with knowing something logically and experiencing it emotionally. By staying with the confusion she was feeling, she began to sort out her reaction to my suggestion. I like how she did her own therapy process through her writing. The letter itself suggested how far she had come in her therapy as she persistently struggled to get herself into a better place.

This time Dorothy didn't have to run very far or isolate herself to walk through the pain she felt. By now she understood that present-day reactions can be about current situations; they can also be tied to emotional issues from the past. One of her "triggers," issues that could send her into a downward spiral, was a situation that suggested abandonment. Her mode of steering clear of that feeling was to avoid intimacy or to stay in control of the relationship. My suggestion to terminate seemingly came out of the blue, and she wasn't prepared for the emotional impact.

Difficult Issues

I really like the quotation from M. Scott Peck because working through tough issues such as death, separation and abandonment can be incredibly meaningful. Dorothy's strong reaction gave her a chance to reflect on an issue that she had a strong aversion to in the past. Then she wrote a prayer about it and, finally, discussed it with me. Many times those types of issues cannot be worked through the way Dorothy was able to because of abrupt death or betrayal.

Strong Reactions

Dorothy's strong reactions always got my attention. Termination had to be handled in such a way that ending the therapy process would "do no harm" and would not extend the therapy process past the point of its making sense.

In the past Dorothy's way of dealing with abandonment issues was to be the one who moved out faster—to be the one who went away. We worked through her pattern by bringing Dorothy to realize that no one was being abandoned. Our therapy contract identified the goals that spelled out the reasons for continuing therapy.

Patients react variously when the subject of terminating therapy comes up. Some patients try to negotiate not ending the therapy process. Other patients agree to end it, and we mutually move toward closure. Sometimes it is the patient who brings up termination and I do not agree. Terminating therapy can be a defensive move to avoid confronting difficult areas of life.

Hanging in There

The amazing thing is that Dorothy hung in there and let me know what was going on inside. She stayed with her feelings even though they were intense and unmanageable. Staying with her feelings ran counter to what she had done before in her life. Dorothy's process through (instead of around) the discomfort indicated to me that our relationship was a safe one in which to work out the dynamic of abandonment in her life. Without the base of trust we had established, she would not have allowed herself to share the immensity of her reaction.

Therapy is often a microcosm of life. For Dorothy to realize that she could work through this pain instead of running from it helped free her up to apply that part of herself to important relationships in her life.

Standing Appointments

When Dorothy came back to therapy to discuss her reaction to being "terminated," it seemed to mark a turning point in the therapy process. From then on she rarely ever avoided feeling her reactions during session and was expressive and open in ways she had been unable to be before. Dorothy had always been direct and clear in her communication, and now she added to that a dimension of stating her feelings while allowing herself to feel them.

When I remembered her initial fear of coming to therapy, I was amused that she would want a permanent standing appointment even though we both knew she didn't need it. Dorothy still wanted a say in her therapy process, including control over termination. While she had always had that control, it was nice to hear her confidence in asking for something she wanted.

Solitary Places

As Dorothy continued the therapy process, she uncovered areas that she had previously covered up. The solitary places of her life were the shadow sides she preferred to keep hidden, even from herself. The process of integration involves accepting all the parts of who we are. Looking at our so-called demons, giving them a name and exposing them to the light, does much to diminish their control over us.

In therapy we refer to the victim-victimizer cycle. Someone who is abused or hurt, as a child or as an adult, suffers the pain and effects of that abuse. A cycle is initiated that allows the abused person to become abusive. In Christian terms it is passing the sins of one generation onto the next in a way that seems incongruent with the intentions of the people involved.

Thus Dorothy caused confusion and pain in the people she cared about most. She had decided to make amends to the people she had hurt in an attempt to bring an end to negative patterns. No one wants to hurt a loved one. I admire Dorothy's courage to face issues about herself that are unpleasant.

I suggested that she choose a "gentle path" for herself, as she tends to be harder on herself than anyone else could possibly be. I really like Patrick Carnes's use of that term in his book *A Gentle Path Through the Twelve Steps* (1993), which is a workbook for all people in the process of recovery.

The process of looking at the solitary places in life is not a one-stop program. It involves dealing with hurts that you have inflicted on people in the past and taking an inventory each day to make sure you have acted with integrity and within your own personal belief system.

The process of looking through her day proved to be very helpful to Dorothy, since she tended to be overly involved in work or activities. For her a process of staying connected to God, making use of meditation, prayer and writing, helped identify a need to make amends to others or to let them know she was hurt by something they did.

Mind Reading

It was very important that Dorothy learn to communicate when she was hurt. I can't read Dorothy's mind, my wife's mind, my children's or grandchildren's minds. No therapist can read anybody's mind. But sometimes Dorothy really thought I should be able to know what was going on with her without her telling me.

To stay clear in her relationships, she learned to express her needs and her wants. At first it was not easy for Dorothy to say she wanted or needed anything from anyone. When she did begin to ask for what she wanted, she didn't always find support. Someone who changes the game plan in a relationship may not be received with open arms. Others may even try to sabotage efforts to change by insisting (sometimes passively) that things get back to "normal."

Part of Dorothy's venturing into the solitary places of her life meant that she would be more open about whatever was going on inside her with the safe people in her life. Her prayer refers to the energy that it takes to keep things inside. A powerful insight! Keeping our thoughts, feelings and desires under wraps is a heavy price to pay in terms of creativity, love and intimacy.

As Dorothy continued to try out new ways of relating and sharing, she developed a capacity to connect intimately with others. Once that shift occurred, it was hard for her to retreat into a solitary place ever again.

8

A Visible
Difference
—Dorothy—

It was Socrates who asserted that the unexamined life is not worth living. By this time my life had been very thoroughly examined. But was my examined life different in any measurable, qualitative way? Did therapy make a difference in my behavior, my thoughts or my experience of myself? I needed to identify some real changes. Was the process of therapy moving me in any significant directions with my relationships?

Well into the therapy process I wrote a mission statement. This statement expressed my understanding of my self and my purpose. I wanted it to transcend what I was "doing" to address what I was "being."

My opening statement reads,

My purpose is to love God and experience that love in a way that transforms my life on a daily basis. I then extend that process to the people I come in contact with through the gifts God has given me.

I saw my therapy as a vehicle to remove the barriers I had erected that kept me from loving God and experiencing transformation.

My mission statement then focuses on the important relationships in my life. Examining those relationships showed me that the effects of my therapy did indeed extend beyond my therapy sessions.

Whenever I have the opportunity, I will use my gifts to help others heal and become whole in their relationships through my writing, prayer, drama and vocational choices.

I do not use my gifts to exploit others or to enrich myself.

I recognize God as the giver of all my gifts, and I cherish them as such.

One of the most treasured parts of therapy was the encouragement Ralph gave me. He remarked once that my writing could be published. His words ignited a barely remembered passion. Now I try to encourage others whenever I can. I know what a difference encouragement can make.

Ralph once explained to me the concept of "enlightened selfishness." It means doing things that bring you joy and fulfillment, bearing in mind the impact being made on significant others. Understanding this has led me to take better care of myself in the area of vocational needs and desires.

I decided to enroll in graduate school to work toward a master of counseling degree. Over the years I had enrolled in three graduate programs that I did not complete. The chaos in my life always prevented me from concentrating on my education. When I enrolled this time, a few friends checked on me to encourage me, support me and make sure I'm wasn't creating a crisis that would "force" me out of another program.

Therapy helped me crystallize my passion for writing. I write for pleasure and creative expression. Writing expresses who I am and how I feel. For much of my life, it was the only way I could communicate the depth of my feelings. It was a protective and healing source, and the writing was for me. Now I share that part of myself with others.

My mission statement includes the following items in regard to my extended family relationships:

I seek interdependence and intimacy to the extent that others are willing.

I do not try to "fix" anyone, nor do I stay in unhealthy places with them.

I recognize that family members are separate from me while being connected to me through a unique bond.

I extend grace and forgiveness to them as God does for me.

My mother said something to me recently about a situation she handled in a healthy way. She expressed her feelings and thoughts to someone without being defensive. I said I was impressed with her response and the way she took care of herself. She said, "Isn't it amazing that I am changing at my age?"

I replied, "I think it's great. You can do anything you want to."

She went silent for a moment and then said, "It's because of you, you know." What a powerful statement of affirmation! It was unusual because we aren't good at affirming each other in my family.

Extended family is still a tough area for me. We don't know how to connect beyond our own pain, and so we have superficial relationships that paper over broken dreams. Perhaps there will be a time when we offer ourselves to each other, when we will listen and accept responsibility for what we contribute to the isolation.

Regarding my friends, my mission statement affirms the following:

I offer myself to my friends in an open and intimate way.

I receive their openness and I welcome their love.

I am willing to work through challenges in relationships and seek restoration when needed.

I am a friend who is loving, reliable, trustworthy and interdependent.

I have no friendships from my past: no connections from school, college, my first marriage or my young adult years. It's not that I didn't make any friends, but when I had a conflict with someone, I didn't seek to resolve it. I left the conflicted friendship and went on to others.

I had superficial friendships that dissolved because I became bored with them or found them draining. I resented persons who used me as a sounding board for their pains and problems. I never offered any information about myself.

During therapy I worked through a friendship that had ended in anger. My friend Carma and I had several interests in common: church, socializing, family and creativity. After we parted, Carma tried to bridge the chasm between us on several occasions. I rejected her because I didn't know how to work through my anger. I had no model for compromise and restoration, only abandonment and isolation. I used both of them to protect myself.

Our relationship was eventually restored, and I vowed to stop fear from ever again getting in the way of intimacy. While I can't control who will want to go the distance in my friendships, I can control my willingness to work through the "stuck" times.

Ralph helped me by working through some of our own stuck times in therapy. It was an excellent arena for me to try out new skills in a safe environment. There were times when he was clearly frustrated with me and I with him, but he never revoked his support or acceptance of me.

Not all of the friendships that I have now will endure, but my friends and I have a mutual desire to see them through. Do I still want to withdraw sometimes? You bet. Do I still get hurt and angry when someone doesn't understand me? Once in a while. Do the benefits of this created "extended family" outweigh the demands? Absolutely.

My mission statement expresses my understanding of my responsibility to my children as follows:

I will reflect God's parental love to them on a consistent basis.

I will model for them integrity, love, self-esteem and personal responsibility as well as I can.

I will seek their highest good and will encourage their individual gifts, each as a unique child of God.

No one has ever granted me more second chances than my children do. And they don't even know they're doing it. They love me as I grow and they challenge me to be real. I had good relationships with Celeste, Dan and Julie before I began therapy. Now these relationships have become a source of continuing joy and wonderment for me. Being a parent means learning about the uniqueness of each person.

Celeste is bright, funny and intense. Our relationship is better than ever. I have given her permission to talk to me about anything (which she should have had all along). I learn so much from her. She loves looking at sunsets, especially over the ocean. When I see a sunset, I am reminded of how Celeste radiates over her own special horizons. She is as varied as the colors spread over the skyline and as consistent as the sun rising each day.

Dan is calm, friendly, devoted, focused and honest. We are learning to talk to each other about our feelings and struggles. We have to make time to be together and talk because we both have hectic schedules. He is the one who is always there for me. Dan can be assertive. He lets me know he has an opinion and insists on being heard. I'm learning to embrace that part of him instead of trying to control it.

Julie is . . . Julie! She has enjoyed a relatively serene childhood. She clearly states her opinions, feelings and needs. She is sensitive, quiet, bold, intelligent and creative. Her family is a source of security and consistency, and so she feels free to explore her definition of self. She is very literal, which can make her seem critical. She is still becoming Julie, and I'm excited to see her grow. In the past I would have been threatened by that process.

In regard to my husband, John, and me, my mission statement asserts:

I value John and his individual gifts, and I support him as he expresses them outwardly.

I seek to know him and to be known by him intimately on a daily basis.

We share each other's joys and sorrows and extend ourselves as a couple to our other relationships.

We maintain our relationship through love and integrity.

Did therapy hurt or help my marriage? It always helped, even when it felt hurtful, since our relationship was subjected to intense scrutiny. I don't have answers to all of the many questions that marriage raises. Sometimes marriage makes no sense to me. I can't get everything I want and need from one person. And when John needs everything from me, I feel suffocated. The presence of other people in our lives eases the sense of confinement that marriage can generate.

Some of what John and I discovered about each other was hurtful. Old resentments and wounds exploded in therapy sessions. Ralph stood with us as we sorted through the debris. Examining a relationship at such an intimate and revealing level is scary, since there is no guarantee that the relationship will survive the scrutiny.

We have become more responsible, both to ourselves and to each other. We enjoy ourselves separately and together. I think we fight fair most of the time and consequently damage each other less. We still enjoy being together and playing together. We stay married because it makes sense for us, not because church and society say that we should. We like each other—a lot!

In regard to God and me, my mission statement asserts:

I am present with God each day in spiritual union and personal restoration.

I offer my willingness to learn and grow and to be stretched in my awareness of truth.

I receive grace, forgiveness and an abundance of love that flows through me to others in my life.

I cannot experience intimacy without my relationship to God. God seems to draw me into awareness of my spirituality. I don't have to initiate anything other than to be present. I didn't spend much time in therapy actually focusing on my relationship with God, but I got through my toughest moments by writing letters or prayers to God.

I continue working to rid myself of dogmatism and rigid expectations in regard to myself and others. I no longer view my arrogant assertion of opinion as the truth, although I think I'm right. I think God chuckles, just a bit, when I dig in my heels over an issue and refuse to budge: "Dorothy, I'm not going to change regardless of your beliefs, so give us all a break and let go."

Letting go and being real—that is what I continue to do both in therapy and out. Has therapy produced real changes in my life? Yes! It has produced profound changes in every area of my life. Could I have gotten where I am today without therapy? I don't think so. I had to reach out to another person and ask for help.

—*Ralph's Notes*—

Dorothy's mission statement offers a glimpse into the growth that took place in one person during a two-year process of therapy. Her willingness to change was a key factor in the effectiveness of her therapy. Therapy is always helpful when someone is willing to change.

Statements of Identity

Frequently I have patients write an identity statement, which is similar to Dorothy's mission statement. An identity statement includes a description of one's talents and abilities, an explanation of one's purpose in life and an introduction to one's identity. This analysis is a kind of marketing statement that answers the question, If you were trying to sell yourself, what would you spotlight? This kind of exercise celebrates a person's positive qualities instead of looking only at areas that need to be strengthened and worked on. Maintaining a positive focus is an essential aspect of working on problematic areas.

A mission statement sets boundaries and brings together focus and purpose. Corporations, businesses, churches and community agencies have mission statements that define their purpose. Dorothy wrote her mission statement in terms of herself as a child of God. She composed her mission statement independently, not as an assignment.

It is important to celebrate a person's strengths and gifts. Enhanced self-esteem never hurt anyone. It is important for patients to get in touch with their redeeming qualities early in therapy, since a sense of self-worth helps move the therapy process along.

Giving Back

Dorothy is now working as a counselor here at Psychological Counseling Services. It has been over six years since she started therapy and more than four years since she ended it. It is rewarding to observe Dorothy's personal and professional growth.

Enlightened Selfishness

I used the term *enlightened selfishness* with Dorothy to teach her to identify her own wants and needs when making decisions. The first time I introduced that term to her we were discussing the possibility of her applying for a job that interested her and offered benefits that her current job did not. She felt a great deal of pressure to stay in her present position. To decide to pursue a career because she wanted to pursue it was alien to her decision-making process. Having become a wife and mother at age seventeen, she lost her ability as the years passed to identify her own wants and needs.

People who have been programmed not to be selfish sometimes continue to make codependent choices because of their past conditioning. Enlightened selfishness means taking care of others but not at the expense of self. I have worked with too many patients who believed it was their Christian duty to take care of others to the extent that they gave themselves away in the process. Such patients typically become depressed and hostile. They feel angry at the church and at God for having caused the imprisonment they endure. I frequently quote Jesus as having said that the greatest commandment is to love God, neighbor and self. It's usually the self part that gets left out or trampled on in the rush to please God and everyone else.

Enlightened selfishness in a marriage means taking care of self and another person in order to help the team function in a healthy way. Mutual respect and care form the foundation of any relationship. Marriage makes sense when the spouses promote and encourage each other's growth as well as their own.

Never Too Old to Change

I like the part where Dorothy describes her mother's comment about the changes she is making in her life. I am now in my sixties, and I increasingly challenge patients when they say they are too old to change. I guess that's because I know I am capable of continuing to make changes when I need to. I don't want to hear someone who is forty-five or fifty talk about being too old to shift. Any unwillingness to change needs to be addressed very quickly in a therapeutic process if therapist and patient are to get on with the job of actually making changes.

Dorothy's mother attributes her ability to change to Dorothy's beneficial influence. A parent who is able to make such a statement to a child opens a powerful channel of communication between them. Similarly, both of my children have greatly influenced my continuing ability to grow.

Friends

Dorothy worked through some challenges in her attempts to relate to her friend Carma. John, Robin and Carma have given us written permission to tell this story because it exemplifies the positive unintended consequences that can occur through therapy when God is at work in people's lives.

Because of a therapy relationship I had with all four of them at the same time, I was aware that Robin and Carma felt the pain of a broken relationship with John and Dorothy. Each couple was unaware of the other couple's presence at PCS. I knew they were both working through painful issues connected to the others, but I could not bring that up during their sessions. I counseled all of them about some of the same issues at the same time.

Robin and Carma had been John and Dorothy's good friends prior to a situation that resulted in a broken relationship for the four of them. When the relationship ended, John and Dorothy left the church, which they had helped start and of which Robin was the pastor. Dorothy relinquished her friendship with Carma, and they never saw each other in four or five years, even though they continued to live in the same community.

It was a great moment for me as a therapist to hear about the reconciliation that the two couples achieved. Dorothy told me her part of the reconciliation story during therapy, and I heard more of the story at Mountain Park Community Church, which Robin pastors. Dorothy and John are currently attending there.

Therapy found a role to play in the reconciliation process as the couples attempted to make amends. As all involved took time to figure out their role in the breakup of the relationship, therapy provided tools for them to bridge the gap of separation. These tools empowered them to restore this facet of their lives. This is a beautiful example of how therapy becomes another spiritual tool that can be used in the community of faith called the church. They modeled restoration and renewed fellowship through their willingness to risk rejection.

It saddens me that broken relationships in a church frequently drive people out of the church. In this case Dorothy and John left the church when their relationship with Robin and Carma ended. Reconciliation helped these couples renew their friendship as well as continue the ministry of their local church.

Stuck Times

Dorothy states that I helped her work through her stuck times. A therapist often models effective ways to handle relational problems. It's important for a therapist to persist in functioning as a counselor while the patient uses anger and frustration to work through stuck times in therapy. Sometimes the therapist becomes the scapegoat of the moment. Other persons in the patient's life may also serve as scapegoats.

It helped Dorothy to work through relationship issues with me where she felt stuck and then work through similar issues with important people in her life. If there is no place to try new behaviors, we often resort to old patterns that do not work and keep us stuck indefinitely.

Family

As a family therapist, I'm aware that changes can be introduced into a family through changes that occur in one individual. In this case I had the opportunity to see Celeste, John and Dorothy in therapy. Doing therapy made Dorothy a healthier individual and a healthier parent. As Dorothy acquired the ability to celebrate herself, it also became possible for her to celebrate the growth of her children.

John

Dorothy and John had to become more whole as individuals in order to make sense as a couple. They chose therapy as a process to achieve individuation. I strongly believe that the best way to make a decision about a marriage is to grow individually. Sometimes people seem to fear that individual growth will destroy the marriage. And there are times when that occurs, especially when one person is abusive (or both of them are).

A time came in my own marriage when we decided to stay

married because of growth in the marriage. The deciding variable was not that we had once decided to get married but that we now decided to continue being married. As I work with couples, I share my own belief that they need to commit themselves to work on improving things. It is a myth that it takes two people to destroy a marriage. However, it does take two people to build a healthy marriage. Dorothy and John were open to working on their marriage and open to where that might lead.

God

Faith encourages us to be open with ourselves, with God and with each other, as opposed to being self-concealing and dishonest. John and Dorothy are very clear that they are continuing their marital journey and that they expect continuing challenges in their marriage.

I believe therapy helped Dorothy and John's marriage. Therapy benefited my marriage, and it can be therapeutic for any couple caught up in a stressful situation. Therapy means having a candid relationship with someone who doesn't have an ax to grind other than to help that person or couple be "restored to sanity."

In a sense therapy is discipling or mentoring someone who needs a coach or catalyst to achieve change. I have certainly needed that in my own life, and I will remain open to that possibility as long as I live. My most significant coach is God. I am greatly helped by conversations with my wife, my children and my friends. But there have been painful points in my life when my therapists did for me what no one else was capable of doing at that moment. At different times in my life I have needed different therapeutic specialties and thus different therapists. For me it was an experience of reaching out to God for help, as well as reaching out to the therapist, in a joint venture of growth and support.

9

Closure
—*Dorothy*—

As I waited to see Ralph, I went over my agenda for that day's session. I always came in with an agenda. We rarely followed it, but I created one anyway. I suppose it gave me a sense of control or a feeling of security.

I operated from a position of control and organization in many areas of my life. Sometimes this mode was helpful and sometimes it wasn't. The ability to meet deadlines, handle several projects at one time, coordinate events and manage time came from my disciplined side.

But having everything in order and operating according to plan can limit creativity and spontaneity, and it can stunt relationships with people who are not detail oriented. When logic and precision overtake emotion and compassion, you run the risk of becoming an automaton.

Focusing on flexibility and balance would help me avoid overly controlling myself and others. Ironically, those two qualities seemed to fly out the window when I was in a therapy session with Ralph. "Dorothy, hi. Come on back to my office, and I'll meet you there." Ralph greeted me and then stopped in the reception area to check notes and messages.

My appointment that day was at 3:00 p.m., and John and I had one together at 5:00 p.m. I wanted to use my hour to work on personal issues, and I wanted John to have the second hour alone to work on some of his issues. I suspected Ralph wouldn't agree because he wanted John and me to work on some relational issues together.

I generally engaged in small talk until I felt ready to get into a deeper conversation. I suspected that Ralph recognized my behavior as my way of connecting with him without feeling pressured. Ralph never made me feel rushed or patronized. I soon felt safe enough to dig into the real issues.

First I decided to approach the subject of the later appointment. "I know that you probably won't agree [poor posturing on my part], but I want to take a break from joint sessions for a while."

Ralph asked, "Do I have a vote on this?"

"Yes, of course, but let me explain why I think it is a good choice for me." I seemed to have his agreement, although sometimes he listened without committing himself and was hard to read. I decided to give it my best effort. It was very important to me, and I needed to be heard. "I don't want to come back with John," I explained, "because he has eight pages of things he's listed that seem to be about me and our relationship. John is not great at telling me when something bothers him until we are in here with you, and then he lets loose with ten years of accumulated stuff that bothers him. I don't think it's healthy for me to have to sit and listen. I think it would be much better for him to work that out with you, alone, and then bring us back together at a later date."

There, I had presented my case. I felt sure that Ralph would see the logic of my arguments. I was willing to work hard on this marriage, but I needed to give John time to vent his frustrations.

Time to find out if he truly wanted to be married to me. I had had enough of sessions where I felt attacked and vulnerable and where our marriage ended up being in a horrible place. Finally Ralph responded. "I think you definitely should be here for the session with John."

I was stunned! Hadn't he heard me?

"Ralph, it's not safe for me to do that. I really don't want to be here."

"I understand, Dorothy, but I think you need to be here. I want you to come back this afternoon if you can arrange it. You're starting to feel like running away, aren't you?"

Part of me loved how adept Ralph was at picking up my nonverbal cues. But those cues weren't exactly subtle. I had folded my arms, set my jaw and crossed my legs while swinging my foot agitatedly. I decided to give it one more shot.

"Really, I have no intention of doing that. How would you like to listen to your wife rattle off eight pages of complaints against you?"

"Yes, I would want to know what Glenda had to say that required eight pages to put down. Besides, I am sure that one or two things would be valid. Dorothy, if you can arrange your schedule to be back and if you choose to do that, then I will see you at 5:00. If that doesn't work out, we'll meet again at your next appointment."

I appreciated Ralph's directness with me and his willingness to leave the decision with me. Although he was my counselor, only I could make choices about my life. He was consistent in his acceptance of me even when I wasn't ready to deal with something. I didn't feel pressured when he didn't agree with me.

Our time was nearly up, and now I had a dilemma. Part of me felt empowered to come back to the session and work through John's list. I was up to the challenge, and I decided to place my trust in Ralph's determination of how the work should be done. Perhaps this would be one of those breakthrough times that happen in therapy and in life that move us to a deeper awareness of who we are.

The other part of me was too tired to work out the logistics needed to rearrange my schedule. I had to drive home in rush-hour traffic, pick up Julie from her piano lesson, take her home and get myself back out to PCS by 5:00. That meant I would be about fifteen minutes late. It was the end of the day, so I knew Ralph would probably be late getting started.

By that time I was somewhat curious about John's list. I left Ralph a note telling him I would be back and to start without me. When I arrived back at PCS, it was 5:20 and the secretary was still at the front desk. I asked her if John was in with Ralph and if I should join them. She said yes to both questions, so I walked down the hall to his office, knocked on the door and looked in.

"Dorothy, would you mind waiting for a few minutes in the other room? We need to have a few moments to finish."

"OK." I answered. But it wasn't OK at all. It wasn't fine with me because Ralph had been clear about wanting me to be in the session with them. Did that mean I was right and the content of the eight pages was too intense for me to hear? Why did he tell me to come back in the first place? Now I desperately needed to know what was being said. It was so horrible that even Ralph had decided I couldn't be in there.

As I waited by myself, my mind turned to what I felt was a very unfair situation. I felt betrayed and confused, so I started feeling angry. It felt safer somehow. The anger intensified as I sat and waited. Finally the hour was almost up. I had toyed with the idea of getting up and leaving, but I'd worked very hard on not running away. I was determined to stay. I tried to quit feeling angry but was unsuccessful. I continued to feel angry and powerless at the same time.

After I had waited for forty-five minutes, Ralph came out to get me. He smiled and I glared. As I passed him in the hall, he faked a display of fear at my obvious anger. His attempt at levity only made me more furious. The tension in his office was almost unbearable. I had experienced this before, but I thought I had progressed beyond it.

"Dorothy, what is going on with you right now?" Ralph was the one who broke the silence.

"I can't believe that you kept me waiting for forty-five minutes when I didn't want to be here in the first place. I told you I didn't want to be here, but you insisted, and then you didn't even include me in the session." Then I shut down, as I always did when I felt emotional and vulnerable. I couldn't communicate because of the terrible turmoil that was churning inside me. I just couldn't talk.

"Dorothy, I really need you to talk to me. I can't read your mind."

Ralph continued even though I didn't respond. My mind began to wander so I wouldn't feel connected to what was going on in the room. Usually I looked around the room at his books or I thought about something else. Anything to block my emotions. I hated this reaction, but it was all I knew. It was learned behavior, programmed at a very deep level.

Ralph said, "Dorothy, this time I think you're being unfair."

Interesting. He said that he thought I was being unfair, but he did not condemn me as a jerk and terminate me as a patient. That would have been the expected response from my past. His displeasure had to do with my behavior, not with who I was. I liked that.

"Dorothy, would you please look at me for a moment?" I looked at him and listened. "I asked you to come back for this session, and you said you probably couldn't. When I got your note saying you would be late, I called to tell you not to come. I had changed my mind about how I wanted to handle the session." As I listened, I saw the situation in a very different light. He had simply changed his mind about how he wanted to spend that hour. I was wrong to think that he had in some way betrayed me.

When I shut down, I blocked out feedback. It's hardly surprising that I felt abandoned. I could have verbalized that and avoided all of the unnecessary theatrics. At that moment I understood that I could break my customary pattern of tortured silence and express my feelings. I had never done that before—ever. It seemed scary, but I sensed the possibility of freedom. I sensed that God was urging me to break free from my pattern and experience the safety that doing so would bring.

"I'm sorry," I managed to say. "I love you both, and I never intended to hurt you by being silent. I just don't know what else to do." As I began to speak, tears came to my eyes.

Ralph smiled and said, "You're doing it now." When that session ended, my therapeutic relationship with Ralph was ready to be retired.

It had been two years and two months since I first came to Ralph for help. But that season of my life ended, and I began to do life without therapy. I decided to pursue writing and counseling. I love them both and often think about the incredible gift it is to work at something that is enjoyable and fulfilling. My support system—family and friends—sustains me through good and bad times.

When I finally terminated therapy, I wrote letters of closure to Ralph, John and God. I'm in a much better place now. I anticipate being in an even better place in the future. That may happen with therapy or without it, but it excites me to know I can continue to grow as long as I live. I find joy in sharing my story, especially when it moves someone to pursue recovery. I also try to give people a greater understanding of the therapy process.

When I felt ready to terminate my own therapy, I felt a deep sadness. It wasn't the usual panic that I had experienced in the past, and I didn't feel it all the time. I was sad because Ralph would be losing his place in my life. Moreover, I sensed that there was something that hadn't been said between us. Something about the healing that had taken place and what that meant to my life. One day it came to me. I hadn't thanked Ralph or described to him what the past few years had meant to me.

So I composed the following letter of closure to him:

Dear Ralph,

What a peaceful place I'm in here at the Franciscan Renewal Center! It's great to be by myself for a few days. My physical surroundings here in the mountains are lovely. Nature's sounds are amplified by the quiet of this place—the birds singing and the wind whistling through the trees.

I need regular retreats to spend time with myself and with God. I have always enjoyed being alone, but I found myself feeling panicky once I had settled in here at the center. Go figure! I decided to walk until the tension eased. I came to this place with two objectives. One was to ask God what I needed to look at in my life in order to distinguish between what is authentically me and what is only protective covering. It's the same process we worked on in therapy. The more I enjoy being with me, the more I enjoy and celebrate being with others.

My second objective was to write down the feelings and thoughts that I have about our time in therapy these past two years. To help me bring closure to our relationship and to tell you how tremendously important you and the process have been in my life.

During the two weeks since we terminated our therapy relationship, great waves of grief have engulfed me. These waves find me when I hear someone describe a breakthrough in therapy, when I have an insight that I want to share with you and when conflict threatens and I need your help.

The greatest gift you gave to me in therapy was your being

present with me. Staying with me through the anger, the silences, the panic, the withdrawal and the joy. Not taking any of it personally and not judging me, even when much of my anger was directed at you.

Often you carefronted me and mirrored back to me my dysfunction. Your willingness to enter into my pain enabled me to let it go. Many times I thought, *Now I've done it. I've pushed Ralph too far. This time he'll tell me he's had enough.* But that never happened, and somewhere along the way I lost that fear of abandonment.

You shared yourself with me in therapy. You didn't wrap yourself in your professionalism. You made mistakes! What a gift to me! What a role model and mentor! You have grown beyond perfectionism in your own life. You don't need to be perfect or right. You can make mistakes and you can grow.

Finally, you gave me friendship. I treasure having you in my life, and I enjoy the intellectual and emotional exchange we share. God gave me such a gift when he directed me to you. Thank you for being part of my journey. Thank you for letting me be part of yours.

Your friend,
Dorothy

I wrote the following letter of closure to my husband, John:

Dear John,

I am writing letters to Ralph and to God. I am writing you a letter too, since you have been an active participant in my recovery. Therapy is tough work and can generate times of uncertainty for everyone involved.

You had to watch as I experienced pain and frustration. Sometimes I isolated myself from you even as you stood by me. Often I didn't know what was wrong, and in my confusion I lashed out at you. I'm sorry for that.

Then we struggled together. The relationship between us had to change or it would die. It was a frightening, angry time for both of us. I wasn't sure I wanted you to change because then I would have to let go of my anger. You began your own recovery, and God blessed us with a miracle. Our marriage is a miracle, and I do love you. You are a loving, nurturing father to our kids. It's difficult to jump into the lives of half-developed children. You continue to grow in that area, and I'm grateful. With Julie you give at least as much emotional support as I do. You are truly gifted.

Our time in therapy excised the infected areas of our togetherness and led to healing and wholeness.

You have grown up emotionally in many ways. You accept responsibility now instead of running from it. You are dependable and trustworthy. I want you in my life, as my husband, for as long as we live. I love no one else as I love you. What we have is real and enduring and not perfect. I like that! Thanks for encouraging me to be separate in our togetherness!

I love you,

Dorothy

Finally, I wrote a letter to God:

Dear God,

How do I begin to thank you for the grace you've extended to me in my life? You formed me and gifted me with talents and purpose even before I experienced life. You remained intimately involved in my life as my creator and Lord. You continue to share who you are through your Spirit in ways that I can comprehend with my finite mind.

I asked you to bring healing to my life and to move me into a feeling relationship with you two years ago. I had a deep yearning to experience you in a more connected, intimate way. I didn't have an answer. I only had an intense need for you.

You brought me to a place of healing. A place where you interacted with Ralph and me on a weekly basis in an incredible way. You didn't give me the answer I wanted, and fear kept me in chains for a long time. But you gave me space to overcome the fear, and you walked with me through it.

How carefully you introduce me to challenging experiences! How gentle you are as I throw up barriers to intimacy in my life! How accepting and forgiving you are!

You are the light of love's flame that radiates throughout my being and connects with that light in each person. It is fathomless yet available. Now I can see that light in others. Sometimes it is barely a flicker, but it's there. As long as it continues to flicker, there's hope.

You have given me opportunities to share my miracle of healing with others. For a while I did not let anyone into that place, not even family. Now I'm glad to share with anyone who needs to hear. It's as though you are saying to me, "Return home and tell how much God has done for you." So I've returned. My therapy time is over for now, and I am available to whatever path you draw me toward. It's easy now to let you be God in my life.

I adore you,
Dorothy

—*Ralph's Notes*—

When people come to therapy in crisis, the initial therapeutic goal is to "stop the bleeding" and make life manageable. When therapy is ongoing or there is no crisis, "what to talk about" may not be as clear to the patient. An agenda can be an effective tool. Patients list possible areas of concern in their lives, which give us a jumping-off point in our sessions.

Dorothy and I often started with her agenda, choosing the item from her list that was most pressing at the moment. She arranged the items on her list in order of difficulty. It looked something like this:

1. Tell Ralph the book he recommended was very helpful.
2. Ask Ralph what he thinks about my job opportunity.
3. Mention that the small group at church is going great.
4. I need to talk to a coworker about a concern at work.
5. I'm still bothered by some of my thoughts.

I tried to focus on the item that troubled her most. Sometimes she wanted to retreat to a less intimidating topic. Even if she was not willing to pursue a topic at that particular time, bringing it up opened the door for us to look at it later. Sometimes I pushed her to stay with a topic even though she felt uncomfortable with it. And sometimes she just said no.

Another strategy that helped get the ball rolling was a review of her homework assignments. If no homework had been assigned, I might ask, "What is the best thing going on in your life? What is the worst?" I tried to focus our effort on the areas of greatest pain. I also made a point of looking at the best thing going on in her life in order to help provide a base of hope.

Expectations

We all have expectations. They are the things we anticipate or think likely to occur. Dorothy had expectations about the list John brought to therapy. I had expectations about who should be in that second session. John had expectations about the session design. When expectations are not met or when they clash, opportunities arise to respond in different ways, optimally in ways that benefit everyone.

I wanted Dorothy to come back for the session with John to avoid the appearance that I might be colluding with either one of them as individuals. I wanted to be helpful to them as individuals and as a couple. Since John expected Dorothy to be there, I didn't want us to change that "mini-contract" when John didn't have a vote in the process.

I thought it was more helpful for Dorothy to confront her anxiety than to let her anxieties control her decisions. It made more sense for her to deal with the reality of the list than to run away from what she expected John to present. It was important for her not to make assumptions about his list.

Come Here, Go Away

Dorothy had a tendency to flee anxiety, literally. She left town at times, she quit counseling, or she detached herself from the process as opposed to staying with it. I wanted her to work through the pain in this case in order to find out what would happen when she did not run. As her therapist, I respected the fact that she chose to stay and thereby broke her pattern of emotionally detaching in the face of fear or anger. If I hadn't been present, she probably would have run away from that confrontation.

Frustration

I knew Dorothy didn't like my noncompliance with her request to change the format of her later session. Her intense glare communicated frustration and/or anger. When Dorothy was upset, she became less flexible and more dogmatic.

I saw myself as Dorothy's coach, trying to help her make the best decisions for her life. I helped her compare what might happen if she left with what might happen if she came back for her second session. I encouraged her to identify what outcome would be in her best interest. I assured her that she had the freedom to choose against coming back. I only hoped that she would make the decision that was best for her at this point in the therapeutic process.

At times I had no idea what made the most sense for Dorothy. Then I saw my role as trying to help her think about options and feel comfortable with her decisions. This dynamic differs from trying to help her break habituated, destructive patterns. I believed that Dorothy needed to stay with this situation and work through it in order to find out there was life on the other side, not catastrophe.

Miscommunication

I received a message that Dorothy had decided to come back for the second session but would be late. I had already begun working with John. The infamous "list" turned out to be personal issues for John that did not involve Dorothy. I felt the responsibility to continue with him in some individual work. I tried to reach Dorothy to tell her that she didn't need to come back after all, but I only succeeded in leaving a message on Dorothy and John's answering machine. She never got that message. Thus a series of mundane events resulted in a lot of emotion. It also provided a springboard for growth during a session.

Dorothy became frustrated and impatient as she waited for John and me. I decided to deal with John's emotions at the moment and with Dorothy's emotions in a little while. John's deep level of hurt was my primary concern at that moment. I needed to continue dealing with him individually.

By the time Dorothy came into the session, little time was left. I made it clear I needed Dorothy to talk so we could deal with what was going on inside her. She was upset with me. I believed Dorothy intended to be fair, but in this situation, I thought her reaction was contrary to that intent. She was being unfair to herself, to John, to me. I saw this as an opportunity for her to break a pattern that she also used with John. I didn't want the session to end with that pattern prevailing in therapy.

Dorothy's frustrated reaction worried me, and I knew I needed help. I silently prayed for help as I clarified Dorothy's options at that moment, which included letting the silence continue, carefronting Dorothy about her withdrawal, ending the session without resolution or trying to help her shift gears.

I chose to carefront her about the chaos she had created. I depended on Dorothy's decision to change gears. I think John benefited by observing me as I tried to get Dorothy to open up. For John, it was a teachable moment.

Finally Dorothy responded. It was a critical moment in her therapy that allowed us to confront patterns that constituted negative "life scripts." She saw that verbalizing her thoughts and feelings could overcome her instinct to isolate or run away.

When Dorothy said she was sorry, John reacted with surprise. It wasn't easy for Dorothy to "be wrong." She went to great lengths to do things right. She felt vulnerable and open to judgment if she didn't cover all the bases. In that moment, John realized that Dorothy was truly committed to changing patterns of behavior that were self-defeating and hurtful to them both.

Releasing the Tears

Dorothy seldom allowed herself to cry. Her tears had turned to angry silence and defensiveness long ago. Dorothy's tears were a significant statement of her desire to risk vulnerability with John and me.

The feelings and tears flowed together. Dorothy became open and vulnerable instead of shutting us out and isolating. As Dorothy cried, I asked her, "What are your tears about? What do your tears mean?" Asking her to speak about her tears helped her stay with her feelings. She could talk about the pain of the moment and stay out of her tendency to intellectualize. Tears were a therapeutic window of opportunity in which Dorothy, John and I shared a softer side of Dorothy.

When Dorothy cried, tears came to my eyes too. I feel great empathy when tears are a breakthrough that is accompanied by enormous pain.

Letters

Dorothy's letter to me was helpful and illuminating. Most people do not initiate contact with me after therapy is over, and thus the letter from Dorothy was tremendously meaningful. It was good to know that she was doing well and finding resources in other people and God as she continued her journey. Dorothy closes the letter by referring to herself as my friend. When I read that, I thought about my relationships with my own therapists. Two of them have passed away. The others remain friends in the deepest sense of the word.

Dorothy's letter to John is powerful. In it she signals her commitment to living in sustained intimacy with him. Both of them recognize the separateness that is an essential component of their togetherness.

Dorothy's letter to God speaks of the intimacy that she finds in that supremely important relationship. God was always at the center of the therapy process. The paradox of her search for intimacy with God was resolved as she became known to herself and to others.

Finally, I would like to share a letter I wrote to Dorothy:

Dear Dorothy,

I'm always amazed at how much I learn about myself in doing therapy with patients. I learned a great deal as I worked with you in a relationship-centered therapy mode.

Dorothy, I believe we are both impatient people. I recognize what an effort it was for you to persevere through those times when your very vocal "minority stockholder vote" urged you to run from therapy and your marriage.

I learned a lot from you about integrating therapy and religious faith. The prayers to God that you wrote, especially, provided great windows into your soul and moved the therapy process along.

Although we don't give certificates of graduation from PCS, it means a great deal to me to know that you continue in your personal growth. Therapy can only be helpful when the patient is willing to work at it. You have certainly done that. You have enormous talents that will enable you to continue improving the recipe for yourself and your relationship with God, John, family and friends.

Your ex-therapist, friend and colleague,

Ralph

Appendix

How to Find a Therapist
—Dorothy—

How did I find a therapist? I found Ralph when I attended a seminar at the church I was attending in summer 1992. "An author who went through therapy and is now a therapist is making a presentation at a seminar at church next week. Let's go. I'm interested in her book and her story," I suggested to my sister Barbi.

"Why?"

"I think she's speaking about some trauma she experienced as a child, and about her recovery. It should be interesting," I explained. I felt drawn to the seminar for some reason, perhaps because I had always been fascinated by true-life stories. I liked to read about personal struggle and triumph. Someone's response to tragedy or great joy interested me.

Part of my interest in other people's stories stemmed from my own inability to share personal information. I wanted to see if the speaker was real and transparent. I needed to hear how she handled the damage from her past. Many people I knew were struggling with their past, and I felt powerless to help or respond to them.

Barbi and I arrived a few minutes early and headed for two empty seats. People milled around in the back of the room, looking over book displays and chatting. "Come on, Barbi, let's sit down. We can look at the books later." I pulled her toward the left side of the room up front. We were avid readers, so I'm sure she wondered why I hadn't stopped to assess the literature.

"OK, but I'm still trying to figure out why we're here," came her puzzled reply.

Our pastor moved toward the front of the room. As he did, people scurried for seats and then became quiet. I looked around, trying to catch sight of the speaker. She sat in the front row across the aisle, looking attractive and polished. I sat two rows back from the front, which was two rows farther back than I usually sat. My sister eyed me with a look that asked, "Now what?"

"Welcome to this very special evening. I have the privilege of introducing to you the person who will be introducing our guest speaker. I've known him for a long time."

The only person who seemed to be reacting to the pastor's introduction was a man sitting across the aisle from me. Leaning forward in his seat, he laughed as he listened to the introduction, clearly enjoying a joke the pastor made about him. He appeared enthusiastic and kind. What I noticed most about him was the ease with which he related to others.

"Please help me welcome Dr. Ralph Earle."

The completed introduction gave me a name and a profession to link to the person: Ralph Earle, psychologist, author and friend of my pastor. I kept that information logged in my brain for future reference. Not that I thought I'd ever need a psychologist, but I could suggest him to anyone who did.

Six months later I found myself in my pastor's office inquiring about Dr. Earle. I wanted to check him out because I thought possibly, maybe, sometime, when I was really old, I might see him. My pastor spoke highly of Dr. Earle on a personal level and a professional level.

After I explained to my pastor why I wanted to see a psychologist, I asked for Dr. Earle's phone number. "Do you need to be accountable to someone about making that call?" my pastor asked. He must have sensed my fear and anxiety about actually setting an appointment.

"I think that would be a good idea," I responded.

"When do you intend to call him?" he gently pushed.

"It's Christmas, so I'm sure he will be booked solid until the first of the year. I'll call then."

"I'm fairly sure his phone is working even if he is booked, so how about this afternoon?" came his counterproposal. Even making a phone call to set an appointment filled me with dread, but I agreed. Having succeeded in identifying the "perfect" therapist, I made the call.

"You've reached Psychological Counseling Services. We are away from our phones between 12:00 p.m. and 2:00 p.m. If this is an emergency . . . " An answering machine! I finally worked up enough nerve to call and then I got an answering machine. Maybe it was an omen. Would my pastor accept an attempted call as fulfilling my end of the bargain? I would try again at 2:00. If I didn't get through, I would wait until the first of the year.

"Psychological Counseling Services, may I help you?"

"Yes, I'd like to make an appointment with Dr. Earle," I croaked into the phone.

"Certainly. Which Dr. Earle would that be?" I was stumped. The receptionist noticed my hesitance and tried to help me. "We have two Dr. Earles in this office—a father and a son."

That helped a little, although the one I saw could have been either. "The Dr. Earle I am referring to is an author." *Please let only one of them be a writer,* I silently prayed.

"That would be Dr. Ralph Earle. If you are making your first appointment, I need some information from you." We talked through some initial information such as name, address, insurance and appointment times. "We have an opening next Monday at 9:00 a.m. Would that work for you?"

I felt a sense of accomplishment at having set up the appointment, even as I began to think up ways I could back out at the last minute if I decided to. That is how I found my therapist, Ralph. There are as many ways to find a therapist as there are ways for a therapist to be found.

—Ralph—

I happened to be at the seminar where Dorothy first saw me as a result of poor scheduling. Attending the seminar meant that I had to work on Friday night, and I disliked working on Friday nights. I have a habit of committing myself to doing something a few weeks in the future, which turns out to interfere with my guarded relaxation time.

The Thursday night before the seminar I looked at my schedule for the next day and realized I had tripped myself up by agreeing to introduce a friend and colleague at a local church. Friday morning I got up feeling a bit angry over my day. Friday's schedule began with a patient hour at 6:15 a.m., earlier than usual. Most days my patient hours began at 7:00 a.m. Now I had to start at 6:15 in the morning and continue into the evening at a church. I was peeved at me.

My workday went by quickly, as usual. In the evening I went to the church. Several things happened to make the evening worthwhile. First, I enjoyed a funny introduction made by the pastor of the church. Second, I enjoyed the presentation. Third, a serendipity occurred—Dorothy's first appointment evolved from that evening.

As a therapist, I never know what may come from presentations, chance meetings or any other situations I find myself in. Name recognition helps keep a private practice strong. I keep up speaking engagements, radio and TV because I know there are always people in the audience who need to do some therapy and may subsequently seek me out.

Dorothy spent a great deal of time researching the subject of therapy, including individual therapists and office locations. Each therapist and each patient has an individual personality and unique ways of relating during the therapy session. Knowing what to expect does not always translate into a good fit between therapist and patient. Dorothy had to experience me as her therapist to determine whether or not we made sense as a doctor-patient team.

Dorothy and I offer the following tips to aid you as you search for a therapist:

1. Locate a "satisfied customer" of the therapist and listen to that person describe the therapy experience.

2. Interview two to four therapists and base your final decision on personal contact. Finding a therapist in the telephone book or through the classified ads is probably not the best way to go.

3. Ask clergy, physicians or other professionals for names.

4. Definitely ask therapists about areas of specialization. State regulatory boards maintain information regarding specific areas of expertise such as family therapy or sex therapy.

5. Question therapists about their religious preferences and whether or not they are open to differing beliefs.

6. Inquire about fees. They usually vary with the therapist and the type of service rendered. At the present time at PCS we have sliding scales that vary from $20 to $200 per hour. It is important to be straightforward with the therapist about fee structure. It is always OK to ask for a reduction according to personal needs, although some therapists do not offer a sliding scale.

7. Call our office and ask for possible contacts in your area if you need a resource and find yourself unable to connect through local sources.

8. Be assertive about your needs and be clear about your expectations. Find a therapist who feels comfortable working with you as a patient. No one therapist has all the answers.